Say It Right in JAPANESE

**Easily Pronounced
Language Systems, Inc.**

INFINITE Destinations, ONE Pronunciation System

D0181042

McGraw·Hill

New York   Chicago   San Francisco   Lisbon   London   Madrid   Mexico City
Milan   New Delhi   San Juan   Seoul   Singapore   Sydney   Toronto

The **McGraw·Hill** Companies

Library of Congress Cataloging-in-Publication Data

Say it right in Japanese / by Easily Pronounced Language Systems.
   p.   cm. — (Say it right)
   ISBN 0-07-146920-6
   1. Japanese language—Pronunciation.

PL543 .S39   2006
495.6'81—dc22   2006044985

5 6 7 8 9 10 11 12 13 14 15 16 17   LBM/LBM   0 9 8

ISBN 0-07-146920-6

McGraw-Hill books are available at special quantity discounts to use as premiums and sales promotions, or for use in corporate training programs. For more information, please write to the Director of Special Sales, Professional Publishing, McGraw-Hill, Two Penn Plaza, New York, NY 10121-2298. Or contact your local bookstore.

Also available:

Dígalo correctamente en inglés (Say It Right in English)
Say It Right in Chinese
Say It Right in French
Say It Right in German
Say It Right in Italian
Say It Right in Spanish

Author: Clyde Peters
Illustrations: Luc Nisset

Acknowledgments

Betty Chapman, President, EPLS Corporation
Priscilla Leal Bailey, Senior Series Editor

This book is printed on acid-free paper.

CONTENTS

INTRODUCTION

The SAY IT RIGHT FOREIGN LANGUAGE PHRASE BOOK SERIES has been developed with the conviction that learning to speak a foreign language should be fun and easy!

All SAY IT RIGHT phrase books feature the EPLS Vowel Symbol System, a revolutionary phonetic system that stresses consistency, clarity, and above all, simplicity!

Since this unique phonetic system is used in all SAY IT RIGHT phrase books, you only have to learn the VOWEL SYMBOL SYSTEM ONCE!

The SAY IT RIGHT series uses the easiest phrases possible for English speakers to pronounce, and is designed to reflect how foreign languages are used by native speakers.

You will be amazed at how confidence in your pronunciation leads to an eagerness to talk to other people in their own language.

Whether you want to learn a new language for travel, education, business, study, or personal enrichment, SAY IT RIGHT phrase books offer a simple and effective method of pronunciation and communication.

PRONUNCIATION GUIDE

Most English speakers are familiar with the Japanese word **Banzai**. This is how the correct pronunciation is represented in the EPLS Vowel Symbol System.

All Japanese vowel sounds are assigned a specific non- changing symbol. When these symbols are used in conjunction with consonants and read normally, pronunciation of even the most difficult foreign word becomes incredibly EASY!

On the following page are all the EPLS Vowel Symbols used in this book. They are EASY to LEARN since their sounds are familiar. Beneath each symbol are three English words which contain the sound of the symbol.

Practice pronouncing the words under each symbol until you mentally associate the correct vowel sound with the correct symbol. Most symbols are pronounced the way they look!

THE SAME BASIC SYMBOLS ARE USED IN ALL SAY IT RIGHT PHRASE BOOKS!

EPLS VOWEL SYMBOL SYSTEM

Ⓐ
Ace
Bake
Safe

EE
See
Feet
Meet

Ⓘ
Ice
Kite
Pie

Ⓞ
Oak
Cold
Sold

(oo)
Cool
Pool
Too

(ĕ)
Men
Red
Bed

(ah)
Mom
Hot
Off

Most of the above Vowel Symbols will also appear in oval form (shown below). This is a simple way to remind you to stretch this sound slightly.

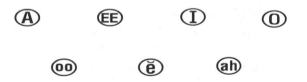

In Japanese, elongation of a vowel sound can change the meaning of a word!

EPLS CONSONANTS

Consonants are letters like **T**, **D**, and **K**. They are easy to recognize and their pronunciation seldom changes. The following pronunciation guide letters represent some unique Spanish consonant sounds.

Ŗ   Represents a unique Japanese sound that falls somewhere between an English **r** and an English **l** sound. Round the tip of your tongue then slightly tap it against the ridge at the top of the front teeth. Mastering the Japanese **r** will take some practice. Have a Japanese-speaking person pronounce these words for you.

KY Represents a sound like the **cu** in **cu**te.

NY Sounds like the **n** in me**nu**.

F   Sounds like the **wh** in **who**. In Japanese, you don't touch your upper teeth to your lower lip to pronounce this letter. Think of it as a cross between an F and an H.

PRONUNCIATION TIPS

- Each pronunciation guide word is broken into syllables. Read each word slowly, one syllable at a time, increasing speed as you become more familiar with the system.

- Japanese is not a tonal language and, in general, native Japanese speakers tend to stress all syllables equally with a tendency to decrease the stress on the last syllable.

- Most symbols are pronounced the way they look!

- Remember that in Japanese, vowel sounds can be pronounced in a short, crisp manner or in a drawn-out manner.

- The oval symbols remind you to lengthen the duration of a vowel sound slightly. This is very important and should not be ignored.

- In Japanese, elongation of a vowel sound can change the meaning of a word!

- Another point to remember is that whenever double consonants appear in a Japanese word they must each be pronounced distinctly. Notice how the **d**'s are pronounced in goo**d d**ay.

ICONS USED IN THIS BOOK

 ## KEY WORDS

You will find this icon at the beginning of chapters indicating key words relating to chapter content. These are important words to become familiar with.

 ## PHRASEMAKER

The Phrasemaker icon provides the traveler with a choice of phrases that allows the user to make his or her own sentences.

Say It Right in JAPANESE

ESSENTIAL WORDS AND PHRASES

Here are some basic words and phrases that will help you express your needs and feelings in Japanese.

Hello / Good afternoon (till about 5 PM)

Konnichi wa

KON-NEE-CHEE Wah

Although the Japanese do not have an exact equivalent of **hello**, **konnichiwa** is the most common greeting.

How are you? (Are you well?)

Ogenki desu ka?

O-GEN-KEE DES-Kah

Yes, I'm well.

Ee, okagesama de.

EE O-Kah-GE-Sah-Mah DE

Good morning (till about 10 AM)

Ohayō

O-Hah-YO

Good morning (more polite)

Ohayō gozaimasu

O-Hah-YO GO-ZI-MahS

Good evening (after sundown)

Konban wa

KON-BaN Wah

Good night

Oyasumi nasai

O-Yah-Soo-MEE Nah-SI

See you later. (informal)

Ja mata.

Jah Mah-Tah

See you again tomorrow.

Mata ashita.

Mah-Tah ahSH-Tah

Good-bye

Sayonara

Sah-YO-Nah-Rah

Yes	No	Maybe
Hai	Iie	Tabun
H①Ⓘ	ⒺⒺ-ⓔ̃	Tⓐⓗ-BⓞⓞN

Please (go ahead)

Dozo

DⓄ-ZⓄ

Please. (after asking for something)

...o kudasai

...Ⓞ Kⓞⓞ-Dⓐⓗ-SⓘⒾ

Excuse me

Sumimasen

Sⓞⓞ-MⒺⒺ-Mⓐⓗ-Sⓔ̃N

I'm sorry

Gomen nasai

GⓄ-Mⓔ̃N Nⓐⓗ-SⓘⒾ

Thanks (very informal)

Dōmo

DⓄ-MⓄ

Thank you

Dōmo arigatō

DⓄ-MⓄ ⓐⓗ-RⒺⒺ-Gⓐⓗ-TⓄ

I'm a tourist.

Watashi wa kankō kyaku desu.

Wah-Tah-SHEE Wah Kahn-KO
KYah-Koo Dĕs

Prounounce **ky** like the **c** in **cu**te.

I don't speak Japanese.

Nihongo ga dekimasen.

NEE-HON-GO Gah Dĕ-KEE-Mah-Sĕn

Do you understand English?

Eigo ga wakarimasu ka?

A-GO Gah Wah-Kah-Ree-MahS-Kah

I understand.

Wakarimashita.

Wah-Kah-Ree-MahSH-Tah

I don't understand!

Wakarimasen!

Wah-Kah-Ree-Mah-Sĕn

Please repeat.

Mo ichido itte kudasai.

MO EE-CHEE-DO EET-Tĕ
Koo-Dah-SI

FEELINGS

I can do (it).

Dekimasu.

Dĕ-KEE-Mah̩S

I cannot do (it).

Dekimasen.

Dĕ-KEE-Mah̩-SĕN

I like this.

Kore wa suki desu.

KO-Rĕ   Wah̩   SKEE   DĕS

I don't like this.

Kore ga suki de wa arimasen.

KO-Rĕ   Gah̩   SKEE   Dĕ   Wah̩   ah̩-REE-Mah̩-SĕN

I have.

Motte imasu.

MOT-Tĕ   EE-Mah̩S

I don't have.

Motte imasen.

MOT-Tĕ   EE-Mah̩-SĕN

I'm hungry.

Watashi no onaka ga sukimashita.

Wah-Tah-SHEE NO O-Nah-Kah Gah
SKEE-MahSH-Tah

I'm thirsty.

Watashi nodo ga kawakimashita.

Wah-Tah-SHEE NO-DO Gah
Kah-Wah-KEE-MahSH-Tah

I'm lost.

Michi ni mayotteimasu.

MEE-CHEE NEE Mah-YOT-Tĕ-MahS

We are lost.

Watashitashi wa michi ni mayotte masu.

Wah Tah-SHEE-Tah-SHEE Wah
MEE-CHEE NEE Mah-YO-Tĕ MahS

I'm sick.

Watashi wa byōki desu.

Wah-Tah-SHEE Wah BEE-O-KEE DĕS

I'm in a hurry.

Isoide imasu.

EE-SO-EE-Dĕ EE-MahS

INTRODUCTIONS

Use the following phrases
when meeting someone
for the first time, both
privately and in business.

**Hello, my name is... (your name) ...
Nice to meet you.**

Konnichiwa...**(your name)**...desu
hajimemashite, dōzo yoroshiku.

KON-NEE-CHEE-Wah...(your name)...DES
Hah-JEE-MEE-MahSH-TEE
DO-ZO YO-ROSH-Koo

Konnichiwa (KON-NEE-CHEE-Wah) may be used
as hello until about 5:00 PM. You may also say:
Ohayō gozimas (O-Hah-YO GO-ZI-MahS)
for good morning and...
Konban wa (KON-BahN Wah) for good
evening.

GENERAL GUIDELINES

Here are some important guidlines to remember when meeting someone for the first time in Japan.

- Bowing is a common greeting used in Japan and it can signify acknowledgment, thanks, humility, or respect.

- It is good practice to bow to show your initiative and interest in Japanese customs.

- Usually first names are reserved for family and close friends.

- Use titles such as **Mr.**, **Ms.**, or **san** with last names.

- You can use **san** when speaking to a man or women, married or single.

- Never use **san** with your name, your spouse's name, or your children's name.

TITLES

In Japan personal titles are very important in both public and private life. Knowing some of these titles is an easy way to address someone politely without knowing his or her name.

Mr. professor or Mr. teacher

Sensei

SⓔN-Sⓐ

Mr. policeman

Omawari san

Ⓞ-Mⓐⓗ-Wⓐⓗ-RⒺⒺ   SⓐⓗN

Mr. driver (taxi)

Untenshu san

ⓄⓄN-TⓔN-SHⓄⓄ   SⓐⓗN

Miss young lady (a single girl)

Ojōsan

Ⓞ-JⓄ-SⓐⓗN

Mrs. wife (for a married woman)

Okusan

Ⓞ-KⓄⓄ-SⓐⓗN

This literally means **Mrs. interior!**

Mr. doctor

Oisha san

Ⓞ-ⒺⒺ-SHⓐⓗ SⓐⓗN

Mr. dentist

Ha isha san

Hⓐⓗ ⒺⒺ-SHⓐⓗ SⓐⓗN

Mr. postman

Yūbinya san

Yⓞⓞ-BⒺⒺN-Yⓐⓗ SⓐⓗN

Mr. lawyer

Bengoshi san

BⓔN-GⓄ-SHⒺⒺ SⓐⓗN

The Japanese equivalent of **Mr.**, **Mrs.**, or **Miss** is **san**. The name is pronounced first and **san** follows.

Bailey **san**   Chapman **san**   Navin **san**

San can also be used with a person's first name:

Michelle **san**   Priscilla **san**   Tracy **san**

Mathew **san**   Brandon **san**

Never use **san** with your own name!

THE BIG QUESTION

Who?

Dare?

D⒜-R⒠

Who is it?

Donata desu ka?

D◎-N⒜-T⒜ D⒠S-K⒜

What?

Nan desu ka?

N⒜N D⒠S-K⒜

What's that?

Sore wa nan desu ka?

S◎-R⒠ W⒜ N⒜N D⒠S-K⒜

What's this?

Kore wa nan desu ka?

K◎-R⒠ W⒜ N⒜N D⒠S-K⒜

When?

Itsu desu ka?

⒠⒠T-S◉◉ D⒠S-K⒜

Where?

Doko desu ka?

D◎-K◎ D⒠S-K⒜

Where is…?

…wa doko desu ka?

…Wah DO-KO DĕS-Kah

Name what you're looking for then say **wa doko desu ka**.

Which?

Dore desu ka?

DO-Rĕ DĕS-Kah

Why?

Naze desu ka?

Nah-Zĕ DĕS-Kah

How?

Dō desu ka?

DO DĕS-Kah

How much does it cost?

Ikura desu ka?

EE-Koo-Rah DĕS-Kah

How long does it take?

Dono gurai kakarimasuka?

DO-NO Goo-RI
Kah-Kah-REE-Mah-S-Kah

ASKING FOR THINGS

The following phrases are valuable for directions, food, help, etc.

I would like….

… o kudasai.

…Ⓞ Ⓚ⓪-Ⓓⓐⓗ-Ⓢ①

Name what you need then say **…o kudasai.**

I need...

...ga irimasu.

…Gⓐⓗ Ⓔ-Ⓡⓔ-ⓂⓐⓗS

Name what you need then say **...ga irimasu.**

Do you have…?

...o motte imas ka?

…Ⓞ MⓞT-Tⓔ̌ Ⓔ-ⓂⓐⓗS-Ⓚⓐⓗ

Name what you need then say **...o motte imas ka.**

PHRASEMAKER

In English we say **I would like coffee**. In Japanese you say **Coffee I would like**. Name what you would like then go to the bottom of the page and say **...o kudasai**.

▸ **(More) coffee...**

(Motto) kōhī...

(MOT-TO) KO-HEE...

▸ **Some water...**

Mizu...

MEE-Zoo...

▸ **Some ice...**

Kōri...

KO-REE...

▸ **The menu...**

Menū...

MEH-NYoo...

...I would like.

... o kudasai.

...O Koo-Dah-SI

PHRASEMAKER

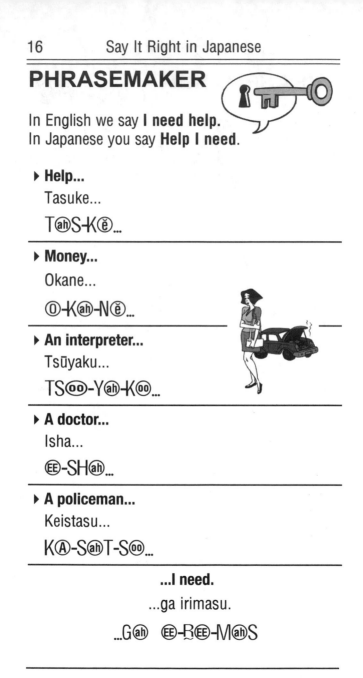

In English we say **I need help.**
In Japanese you say **Help I need**.

▸ **Help...**

Tasuke...

T⒜S-K⒠...

▸ **Money...**

Okane...

Ⓞ-K⒜-N⒠...

▸ **An interpreter...**

Tsūyaku...

TS⒪⒪-Y⒜-K⒪⒪...

▸ **A doctor...**

Isha...

Ⓔ⒠-SH⒜...

▸ **A policeman...**

Keistasu...

KⒶ-S⒜T-S⒪⒪...

...I need.

...ga irimasu.

...G⒜ Ⓔ⒠-RⒺⒺ-M⒜S

PHRASEMAKER

In English we say **Do you have aspirin?** In Japanese you say **Aspirin do you have?** Name what you would like, then go to the bottom of the page and say **...o motte imasu ka?**

▶ **Aspirin...**

Asupirin...

ⓐS-Pⓔⓔ-RⓔⓔN...

▶ **Envelopes...**

Fūtō...

Fⓞⓞ-Tⓞ...

▶ **A Tokyo map...**

Tōkyo chizu...

Tⓞ-KYⓞ CHⓔⓔ-Zⓞⓞ...

▶ **Postcards...**

Hagaki...

Hⓐ-Gⓐ-Kⓔⓔ...

▶ **Stamps...**

Kitte...

KⓔⓔT-Tⓔ̆...

...do you have?

...o motte imasu ka?

...ⓞ MⓞT-Tⓔ̆ ⓔⓔ-MⓐS-Kⓐ

ASKING THE WAY

No matter how independent you are, sooner or later you'll probably have to ask for directions.

Where is…?

...wa doko desu ka?

...WⓇ DⓄ-KⓄ DĕS-KⓇ

Name what you're looking for then say **wa doko desu ka?**

I'm looking for...

...o sagashite imasu.

...Ⓞ SⓇ-GⓇ-SHⓊ-Tĕ Ⓤ-MⓇS

Name what you're looking for then say **o sagashite imasu.**

Is it near?

Chikaku desu ka?

CHⓊ-KⓇ-KⓌ DĕS-KⓇ

Is it far?

Tōi desu ka?

TⓄ-Ⓤ DĕS-KⓇ

I'm lost!

Mayotta!

MⓇ-YⓄT-TⓇ

PHRASEMAKER

In English we say **Where is the restroom?** In Japanese you say, **The restroom, where is it?** In this phrasemaker, name what you are looking for, then go to the bottom of the page and say **...wa doko desu ka?**

▸ **The restroom...**

Otearai..

Ⓞ-Tⓔ-ⓐⓗ-Ⓡ①...

▸ **The telephone...**

Denwa...

DⓔN-Wⓐⓗ...

▸ **The beach...**

Kaigan..

K①-GⓐⓗN...

▸ **The hotel** (name hotel)...

Hoteru...

Hⓞ-Tⓔ-Rⓞⓞ...

...where is it?

...wa doko desu ka?

...Wⓐⓗ Dⓞ-Kⓞ DⓔS-Kⓐⓗ

TIME

What time is it?
Nanji desu ka?

N@N-J㊙ D㊮S-K@

Morning
Asa

@-S@

Noon (12:00 PM)
Ohiru

◎-H㊙-Ŗ㊯

Night
Yoru

Y◎-Ŗ㊯

Today
Kyō

KY◎

Tomorrow
Ashita

@-SH㊙-T@

Yesterday
Kinō

K㊙-N◎

This week

Konshū

K⊙N-SH⊚⊚

This month

Kongetsu

K⊙N-G⊚̃T-S⊚⊚

This year

Kotoshi

K⊙-T⊙-SH⊛

Now

Ima

⊛-M⊛

Soon

Mō sugu

M⊙ S⊚⊚-G⊚⊚

Later

Ato de

⊛-T⊙ D⊚̃

Some day

Itsuka

⊛T-SK⊛

WHO IS IT?

I

Watashi

W@h-T@h-SH€€

You

Anata

@h-N@h-T@h

We

Watashitachi

W@h-T@h-SH€€-T@h-CH€€

Watashitachi is one word.

They

Anohitotachi

@h-N©-H€€-T©-T@h-CH€€

Anohitotachi is one word.

This person

Kono hito

K©-N©   H€€-T©

That person

Ano hito

@h-N©   H€€-T©

THIS AND THAT

This / These

Kore

KO-Re

That / Those (Close to you)

Sore

SO-Re

That / Those (Far from you)

Are

ah-Re

Mine

Watashi no

Wah-Tah-SHEE NO

Yours

Anata no

ah-Nah-Tah NO

The, A (an)

There are no words in the Japanese language that correspond to the English articles **the, a (an).**

USEFUL OPPOSITES

Near	**Far**
Chikaku	Toi
CHEE-Kah-Koo	TO-EE
Here	**There**
Koko	Soko
KO-KO	SO-KO
Left	**Right**
Hidari	Migi
HEE-Dah-REE	MEE-GEE
A little	**A lot**
Sukoshi	Taksan
SKO-SHEE	TahK-SahN
More	**A little**
Motto	Sukoshi
MOT-TO	SKO-SHEE
Big	**Small**
Ōkii	Chīsai
O-KEE	CHEE-SI

Open	Closed
Aiteiru	Shimatteiru
ah-EE-TA-Roo	SHEE-Mah-T-TA-Roo

Cheap	Expensive
Yasui	Takai
Yah-Soo-EE	Tah-KI

Clean	Dirty
Kirei	Kitanai
KEE-RA	KEE-Tah-NI

Good	Bad
ii	Warui
EE	Wah-Roo-EE

Up	Down
Ue (ni)	Shita (ni)
oo-e (NEE)	SHEE-Tah (NEE)

Right
Tadashii
Tah-Dah-SHEE

Wrong
Machigatteiru
Mah-CHEE-Gah-T-TA-Roo

WORDS OF ENDEARMENT

I like you.

Anata ga suki desu.

ⓐ-Nⓐ-Tⓐ-Gⓐ SKⒺ Dⓔ̃S

I love you.

Anata o aishite imasu.

ⓐ-Nⓐ-Tⓐ Ⓞ Ⓘ-SHTⓔ̃ Ⓔ-MⓐS

I love Japan.

Nihon ga suki desu.

NⒺ-HⓄ N Gⓐ SKⒺ Dⓔ̃S

I love Tokyo.

Tōkyo ga suki desu.

TⓄ-KYⓄ Gⓐ SKⒺ Dⓔ̃S

I love Yokohama.

Yokohama ga suki desu.

YⓄ-KⓄ-Hⓐ-Mⓐ Gⓐ SKⒺ Dⓔ̃S

WORDS OF ANGER

What do you want?

Nani ga hoshii desu ka?

N@h-N€€ G@h H⊙-SH€€
D⊚S-K@h

Leave me alone!

Kamawa nai de!

K@h-M@h-W@h N① D⊚

Go away!

Attuchi e itte!

@hT-CH€€ ⊚ €€T-T⊚

Stop bothering me!

Jama o shinai de!

J@h-M@h ⊙ SH€€-N① D⊚

Be quiet!

Shizuka ni!

SH€€Z-K@h N€€

That's enough!

Jū-bun desu!

J⊙⊙-B⊙⊙N D⊚S

COMMON EXPRESSIONS

When you are at a loss for words but have the feeling you should say something, try one of these!

Who knows?

Dare mo shirimasen yo?

D@h-R€ M◐ SH€€-R€€-M@h-S€N Y◐

That's the truth!

So desu ne!

S◐ D€S N€

Sure.

Hai.

H①

I don't believe it !

Shinjirarenai!

SH€€N-J€€-R@h-R€-N①

What's happening?

Gokigen ikaga desu ka?

G◐-K€€-G€N €€-K@h-G@h D€S-K@h

I think so!

Hai, so desu!

HĪ SŌ DēS

Cheers!

Kanpai!

Kah N-PĪ

Good luck!

Ganbatte

Gah N-Bah T-Tē

With pleasure.

Yorokonde.

YŌ-RŌ-KŌN-Dē

It's O.K.

Daijobu docu.

DĪ-JŌB DēS

What a shame! / That's too bad.

Zannen desu!

Zah N-NēN DēS

Well done! Bravo!

Banzai!

Bah N-ZĪ

USEFUL COMMANDS

Stop!

Tomete kudasai!

TO-ME-Te Koo-Dah-SI

Go!

Itte kudasai!

EET-Te Koo-Dah-SI

Wait!

Chotto matte kudasai!

CHOT-TO Mah T-Te Koo-Dah-SI

Hurry!

Isoide kudasai!

EE-SI-EE-De Koo-Dah-SI

Slow down!

Joko shite kudasai!

JO-KO SHEE-Te Koo-Dah-SI

Come here!

Koko ni kite kudasai!

KO-KO NEE KEE-Te Koo-Dah-SI

Help!

Tasukete

Tah S-Ke-Te

EMERGENCIES

Fire!

Kaji da!

K(ah)-J(EE) D(ah)

Emergency!

Kinkyū!

K(EE)N-KY(oo)

Pronounce **ky** like the **c** in **c**ute.

Call the police!

Keisatsu o yonde!

K(A)-S(ah)T-S(oo) (O) Y(O)N-D(e)

Call a doctor!

Isha o yonde!

(EE)-SH(ah) (O) Y(O)N-D(e)

Call an ambulance!

Kyūkyūsha o yonde!

KY(oo)-KY(oo)-SH(ah) (O) Y(O)N-D(e)

Pronounce **ky** like the **c** in **c**ute.

I need help.

Tasukete.

T(ah)S-K(e)-T(e)

ARRIVAL

Passing through customs should be easy since there are usually agents available who speak English. You may be asked how long you intend to stay and if you have anything to declare.

- Have your passport ready.

- Be sure all documents are up-to-date.

- While in a foreign country, it is wise to keep receipts for everything you buy.

- Be aware that many countries will charge a departure tax when you leave. Your travel agent should be able to find out if this affects you.

- If you have connecting flights, be sure to reconfirm them in advance.

- Make sure your luggage is clearly marked inside and out.

- Take valuables and medicines in carry-on bags.

KEY WORDS

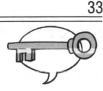

Baggage

Nimotsu

N㉐-M⓪T-S⓪⓪

Customs

Zeikan

Z㉑-K㉕N

Documents

Shorui

SH⓪-R⓪⓪-㉐

Passport

Pasupōto

P㉕S-P⓪ T-T⓪

Porter

Pōtā-san

P⓪-T㉕ S㉕N

Tax

Zeikin

Z㉑-K㉐N

Taxi stand

Takushī noriba

T㉕K-SH㉐ N⓪-R㉐-B㉕

USEFUL PHRASES

Here is my passport.

Watashi-no Pasupōto desu.

W@-T@-SH㋐ N㋔

P@S-P㋔-T㋔ D㋒S

I have nothing to declare.

Shinkokusuru mono ga arimasen.

SH㋐N-K㋔K-S㋵-B㋵

M㋔-N㋔ G@ @-B㋐-M@-S㋒N

I'm on a business trip.

Shigoto no ryokō des.

SH㋐-G㋔-T㋔ N㋔ B㋐-㋔-K㋔ D㋒S

I'm on vacation.

Kyūka des.

KY㋵-K@ D㋒S

Is there a problem?

Mondai ga arimasuka?

M㋔N-D㋑ G@ @-B㋐-M@S-K@

PHRASEMAKER

I'll be staying...

Koko ni...

K⓪-K⓪ N🅴🅴...

▸ **one week**

shu kan imas

SH⓪⓪ K🅰N 🅴🅴-M🅰S

▸ **two weeks**

ni shu kan imas

N🅴🅴 SH⓪⓪ K🅰N 🅴🅴-M🅰S

▸ **one month**

i kagetsu imas

🅴🅴 K🅰-G🅴̃-TS⓪⓪ 🅴🅴-M🅰S

▸ **two months**

ni kagetsu imas

N🅴🅴 K🅰-G🅴̃-TS⓪⓪ 🅴🅴-M🅰S

USEFUL PHRASES

I need a porter!

Pōtā san o onegaishimasu!

PⓄ-Tⓐⓗ SⓐⓗN Ⓞ
Ⓞ-Nⓔ̆-GⒾ-SHⒺⒺ-MⓐⓗS

These are my bags.

Watashi no nimotsu desu.

Wⓐⓗ-Tⓐⓗ-SHⒺⒺ NⓄ
NⒺⒺ-MⓄT-Sⓞⓞ Dⓔ̆S

I'm missing a bag.

Nimotsu ga mitsukarimasen.

NⒺⒺ-MⓄT-Sⓞⓞ Gⓐⓗ
MⒺⒺTS Kⓐⓗ-Rⓔⓔ-Mⓐⓗ Sⓔ̆N

Mitsukarimasen is one word.

Thank you.

Arigatō.

ⓐⓗ-RⒺⒺ-Gⓐⓗ-TⓄ

This is for you.

Kore o dōzo.

KⓄ-Rⓔ̆ Ⓞ DⓄ-ZⓄ

PHRASEMAKER

To say **Where is...?**, name
what you are looking for then go
to bottom of the page and say **...wa doko desu ka?**

▸ **Customs...**

Zeikan...

Z🅐-K🅐N...

▸ **Baggage claim...**

Nimotsu no ukeitorijo...

N🅔🅔-M🅞T-S🅞🅞 N🅞 🅞🅞-K🅐-T🅞-R🅔🅔-J🅞...

▸ **The money exchange...**

Ryōgaejo...

R🅔🅔-🅞-G🅐-🅔-J🅞...

▸ **The taxi stand...**

Takushi noriba...

T🅐K-SH🅔🅔 N🅞-R🅔🅔-B🅐...

...where is?

...wa doko desu ka?

...W🅐 D🅞-K🅞 D🅔S-K🅐

HOTEL SURVIVAL

A wide selection of accommodations are available especially around major tourist areas. Both western style and traditional Japanese inns or (Ryokan) are available. When booking your room, find out what amenities are included for the price you pay.

- Make reservations well in advance and get written confirmation of your reservations before you leave home.

- Always have identification ready when checking in.

- Do not leave valuables or cash in your room when you are not there!

- Electrical items like blow-dryers may need an adapter. Your hotel may be able to provide one, but to be safe, take one with you.

- Tipping is not part of the Japanese culture. The exception would be at first class hotels or ryokan.

- Your hotel front desk can usually assist you with posting mail or packages with private carriers like Federal Express.

KEY WORDS

Hotel (Western-style)
Hoteru

HO-Tē-Roo

Hotel (Japanese-style)
Ryokan

Rēē-O-KahN

Bellman
Bōi

BO-ĒE

Maid
Mēdo

MA-DO

Message
Messēji

Mē-Sē-JĒE

Reservations
Yoyaku

YO-Yah-Koo

Room rate
Heyadai

Hē-Yah-DI

CHECKING IN

My name is…

Watashi wa…desu.

Wᵃʰ-Tᵃʰ-SHᴱᴱ Wᵃʰ

(your name) Dᵉ̃S

I have a reservation.

Yoyaku shite arimasu.

Yᴼ-Yᵃʰ-Kᵒᵒ SHᴱᴱ-Tᵉ̃

ᵃʰ-Rᴱᴱ-MᵃʰS

Have you any vacancies?

Akibeya wa arimasuka?

ᵃʰ-Kᴱᴱ-Bᵉ̃-Yᵃʰ Wᵃʰ ᵃʰ-Rᴱᴱ-MᵃʰS-Kᵃʰ

What is the room rate?

Heyadai wa ikura desu ka?

Hᵉ̃-Yᵃʰ-Dᴵ Wᵃʰ ᴱᴱ-Kᵒᵒ-Rᵃʰ

Dᵉ̃S-Kᵃʰ

Is there room service?

Rūmu sābisu wa arimasuka?

Rᵒᵒ-Mᵒᵒ Sᵃʰ-BᴱᴱS Wᵃʰ

ᵃʰ-Rᴱᴱ-MᵃʰS-Kᵃʰ

PHRASEMAKER

In English we say **I want a room with a bath.** In Japanese you say **A bath...I want a room with.**

▶ **A bath...**

Basu tsuki no heya

BⒶ-SⓊ TSⓊ-KⒸ NⒸ Hĕ-YⒶ...

▶ **A shower...**

Shāwā no heya...

SHⒶ-WⒶ NⒸ Hĕ-YⒶ...

▶ **One bed...**

Hitotsu no beddo...

HⒸ-TⒸT-SⓊ NⒸ BĕD-DⒸ...

▶ **Two beds**

Daburu beddo no heya...

DⒶ-BⓊ-RⓊ BĕD-DⒸ NⒸ Hĕ-YⒶ

▶ **A view**

Ii nagame...

Ⓒ NⒶ-GⒶ-Mĕ...

I want a room with...

...o onegaishimasu.

...Ⓒ Ⓒ-Nĕ-GⒶ-SHⒸ-MⒶS

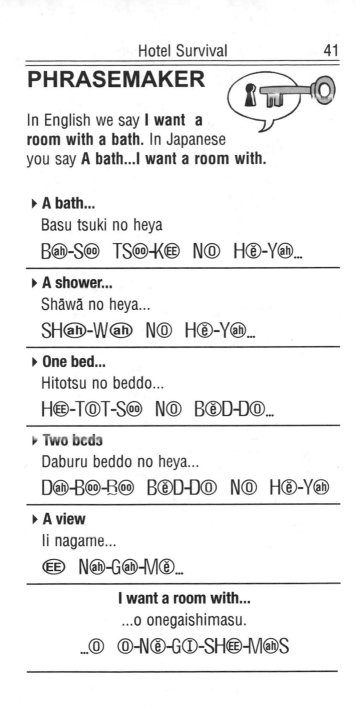

USEFUL PHRASES

What time is checkout?

Chekku auto wa nanji desu ka?

CHⓔK-Kⓞⓞ ⓐⓗ-ⓞⓞ-TⓄ Wⓐⓗ
NⓐⓗN-Jⓔⓔ Dⓔ̄S-Kⓐⓗ

Are there any messages for me?

Watashi ni kotozuke ga arimasu ka?

Wⓐⓗ-Tⓐⓗ-SHⓔⓔ Nⓔⓔ KⓄ-TⓄ-Zⓞⓞ-Kⓔ̃
Gⓐⓗ ⓐⓗ-Rⓔⓔ-MⓐⓗS-Kⓐⓗ

I want to leave this in your safe.

Kore o azukete okitai no desu ga.

KⓄ-Rⓔ̃ Ⓞ ⓐⓗ-Zⓞⓞ-Kⓔ̃-Tⓔ̃
Ⓞ-Kⓔⓔ-Tⓘ NⓄ Dⓔ̄S-Gⓐⓗ

Can you extend my reservation?

Yoyaku o nobasu koto ga dekimasu ka?

YⓄ-Yⓐⓗ-Kⓞⓞ Ⓞ NⓄ-Bⓐⓗ-Sⓞⓞ
KⓄ-TⓄ Gⓐⓗ Dⓔ̄-Kⓔⓔ-MⓐⓗS-Kⓐⓗ

WAKE UP CALL

In English we say **Please wake me at 7:00**. In Japanese you say **At 7:00...please wake me**. Name your wake up time, then go to bottom of the page and say **...ni okoshite kudasai**.

▶ **6:00**

Rokuji

RO-Koo-JEE

▶ **6:30**

Rokuji han

RO-Koo-JEE HaHN

▶ **7:00**

Nanaji

Nah-Nah-JEE

▶ **7:30**

Nanaji han

Nah-Nah-JEE HaHN

▶ **8:00**

Hachiji

Hah-CHEE-JEE

▶ **8:30**

Hachiji han

Hah-CHEE-JEE HaHN

▶ **9:00**

Kuji

Koo-JEE

▶ **9:30**

Kuji han

Koo-JEE HaHN

please wake me at...

...ni okoshite kudasai.

...NEE O-KO-SHEE-Te Koo-Dah-SI

PHRASEMAKER

Here are some items you
may need during your stay.
Name your request, then go to the
bottom of the next page and say **...ga irimasu**.

▸ **A babysitter...**

Komori...

KO-MO-REE...

▸ **A bellman...**

Bōi...

BO -EE...

▸ **More blankets...**

Motto mōfu...

MOT-TO MO -FOO...

▸ **A hotel safe...**

Hoteru no kinko...

HO-TE-ROO NO KEEN-KO...

▸ **Ice cubes...**

Kōri...

KO -REE...

▸ **An extra key...**
Yobi no kagi
YO-BEE NO Kah-GEE...

▸ **A maid...**
Mēdo...
MA-DO...

▸ **The manager...**
Manējā...
Mah-NA-Jah...

▸ **Soap...**
Sekken...
SeK-KeN...

▸ **Toilet paper...**
Toiretto pēpā...
Toy-ReT-TO PA-Pah...

▸ **More towels...**
Motto taoru...
MOT-TO Tah-O-Roo...

...I need
...ga irimasu.
...Gah EE-REE-Mah S

PHRASEMAKER

(PROBLEMS)

In English we say **There is no electricity.** In Japanese you say **Electricity there is no**.

▸ **Electricity...**
  Denki...
  D**ē**N-K**EE**...

▸ **Heat...**
  Netsu...
  N**ē**T-S**oo**...

▸ **Hot water...**
  Oyu...
  O-Y**oo**...

▸ **Light...**
  Raito...
  R**I**-T**O**...

▸ **Toilet paper**
  Toiretto pēpā
  T**oy**-R**ē**T-T**O**   P**A**-P**ah**_

...there is no

...ga arimasen

...G**ah**   **ah**-R**EE**-M**ah**-S**ē**N

PHRASEMAKER

(SPECIAL NEEDS)

In English we say **Do you have an elevator?** In Japanese you say **An elevator... do you have?** Name what you are asking for, then go to bottom of the page and say **...ga arimasu ka.**

▶ **An elevator...**

Erebētā...

ⓔ-Rⓔ-Bⓐ-Tⓐⓗ...

▶ **Facilities for the disabled...**

Shintaishōgaishayō no setsubi...

SHⓔⓔN-T① SH◎-G① SHⓐⓗ-Y◎
N◎ Sⓔ̃T-S◎◎-Bⓔⓔ...

Shintaishogaishayo is one word! The **EPLS** letters are separated to make pronunciation easier.

▶ **A wheel chair...**	▶ **A ramp...**
Kurumaisu...	Keisha-ro...
K◎◎-R◎◎-Mⓐⓗ-ⓔⓔ-S◎◎...	Kⓐ-SHⓐⓗ-R◎...

...do you have?

...ga arimasu ka?

...Gⓐⓗ   ⓐⓗ-Rⓔⓔ-MⓐⓗS-Kⓐⓗ

CHECKING OUT

The bill, please.

Okanjō onegai shimasu.

Ⓞ-Kⓐ🄷N-JⓄ   Ⓞ-Nⓔ-GⒾ
SHⒺⒺ-Mⓐ🄷S

Is this bill correct?

Okanjō wa tadashii desu ka?

Ⓞ-Kⓐ🄷N-JⓄ   Wⓐ🄷   Tⓐ🄷-Dⓐ🄷-SHⒺⒺ
Dⓔ🄴S-Kⓐ🄷

Can I pay with a credit card?

Kurejitto kādo de shiharae masu ka?

Kⓞⓞ-Rⓔ-JⒺⒺT-TⓄ   Kⓐ🄷-DⓄ   Dⓔ
SHⒺⒺ-Hⓐ🄷-Rⓐ🄷-ⓔ   Mⓐ🄷S-Kⓐ🄷

Could you have my luggage brought down?

Nimotsu o shita ni onegaidekimasuka?

NⒺⒺ-MⓄT-Sⓞⓞ   Ⓞ   SHⒺⒺ-Tⓐ🄷   NⒺⒺ
Ⓞ-Nⓔ-GⒾ   Dⓔ-KⒺⒺ   Mⓐ🄷S-Kⓐ🄷

Qnegaidekimasuka is one word!

Can you call a taxi for me?

Takushī o yonde kuremasuka?

TahK-SHEE O YON-Dě
Koo-Rě-MahS-Kah

I had a very good time!

Totemo tanoshikatta desu!

TO-Tě-MO
Tah-NO-SHEE-KahT-Tah DěS

Thanks for everything.

Iroiro ariagatō.

EE-RO-EE-RO ah-REE-Gah-TO

I'll see you next time.

Mata aimashyō.

Mah-Tah O MO-SHO

Good-bye.

Sayōnara.

Sah-YO-Nah-Rah

RESTAURANT SURVIVAL

Japanese cuisine is very popular. You will find a variety of tasty specialties. Mealtimes may be quite different than what you are used to!

- Specialities include teriyaki, sukiyaki, tempura, and sushi. More specialties are listed on pages 54 and 55.

- Traditional Japanese meals consist of a wide array of small dishes.

- Mineral water can be easily obtained from supermarkets and convenience stores; however, tap water is normally safe to drink.

- In Tokyo, there is an abundance of bars and coffee shops, as well as rooftop beer gardens in the summertime.

KEY WORDS

Breakfast

Asa gohan

ah-Sah GO-Hah N

Lunch

Hiru gohan

HEE-Roo-GO-Hah N

Dinner	**Menu**
Yū shoku	Menyū
Yoo SHO-Koo	MēN-Yoo

Waiter	**Waitress**
Uētā	Uētoresu
W A -T ah	W A -TO-Rē-Soo

Western-style food

Yōfū no riyōri

YO -Foo NO REE-O -REE

Japanese-style food

Wafū no riyōri

Wah-Roo NO REE-O -REE

USEFUL PHRASES

I'd like a table for two.

Futari yō tēburu o onegaishimasu.

F⓪⓪-Tⓐⓗ-R㋹㋹ Y⓪

T㋫-B⓪⓪-R⓪⓪ ⓪

⓪-N㋫-G① SH㋹㋹-MⓐⓗS

Separate checks, please.

Okanjyō wa betsu betsu de.

⓪-KⓐⓗN-J⓪ Wⓐⓗ

B㋫T-S⓪⓪ B㋫T-S⓪⓪ D㋫

I'm in a hurry.

Isoide irundesu ga.

㋹㋹-S⓪-㋹㋹-D㋫ ㋹㋹-R⓪⓪N-D㋫S Gⓐⓗ

Do you have an English menu?

Eigo no mēnyū wa arimasu ka?

Ⓐ-G⓪ N⓪ M㋫-NY⓪⓪ Wⓐⓗ

ⓐⓗ-R㋹㋹-MⓐⓗS-Kⓐⓗ

Please bring me…(us).

…o kudasai.

…⓪ K⓪⓪-Dⓐⓗ-S①

Name what you want first then say **…o kudasai.**

I'd like this.

Kore o onegai shimasu.

KO-Bē O O-Nē-GO SHEE-MahS

Can I have a fork?

Hōku wa arimasuka?

HO-Koo Wah ah-BEE-MahS-Kah

I'm hungry.

Onaka ga suite imasu.

O-Nah-Kah Gah Soo-EE-Tē EE-MahS

I'm thirsty.

Nodo ga kawakimashita.

NO-DO Gah
Kah-Wah-KEE-MahSH-Tah

Is service included?

Sābisuryō komi desu ka?

Sah-BEE-Soo-BEE-O
KO-MEE Dēs-Kah

The bill, please.

Okanjyō kudasai.

O-KahN-JO Koo-Dah-SO

JAPANESE SPECIALTIES

The remainder of this chapter will help you order foods you are familiar with. On these pages you will find some common Japanese foods you may want to try!

Sushi
S㊏-SH㊋
Raw fish on top of seasoned rice..

Sashimi
S㋐-SH㋤-M㋤
Fresh fish or shell fish, eaten raw.

Tempura
T㋥M-P㊏-R㋐
Batter-fried seafood and vegetables.

Sukiyaki
S㊏-K㋤-Y㋐-K㋤
Beef and vegetables.

Shabu shabu
SH㋐-B㊏   SH㋐-B㊏
Thinly sliced beef and vegetables cooked in hot broth.

Miso shiru
M㋤-S㊐   SH㋤-R㊏
Soup made from soy bean paste and fish stock, served with most traditional Japanese meals.

Ramen

RAH-MEN

Chinese noodles.

Gohan

GO-HAN

Rice (cooked).

Yakitori

YAH-KEE-TO-REE

Grilled chicken and vegetables on skewers.

Teppanyaki

TEP-PAN-YAH-KEE

Beef, chicken, seafood, and vegetables cooked on a grill in front of you.

Udon

OO-DON

Thick wheat noodles served in broth.

Soba

SO-BAH

Thin buckwheat noodles served in broth or plain.

Yakisoba

YAH-KEE-SO-BAH

Noodles stir fried with meat, vegetables, and a savory sauce.

BEVERAGE LIST

Coffee

Kōhī

KO̅ -HEE

Decaffeinated coffee

Kafein nuki kō-hī

Kah-FAN NOO-KEE KO̅ -HEE

Tea

Ocha (Traditional Japanese green tea)

O-CHah

Tea

Kōcha (Western style)

KO̅ -CHah

with sugar	**with cream**
satō-to	kurīmu-to
Sah-TO̅ TO	KOO-REE-MOO TO

with lemon

remon to

Rē-MON TO

Milk

Miruku

MEE-Roo-Koo

Hot chocolate

Kokoa

KO-KO-ah

Juice	**Orange juice**
Jūsu	Orenji Jūsu
JOO-SOO	O-REN-JEE JOO-SOO

Tomato juice

Tomato Jūsu

TO-Mah-TO JOO-SOO

Coca cola	**Pepsi cola**
Koka kōra	Pepushi kōra
KO-Kah KO-Rah	PEP-SHEE KO-Rah

Water	**Ice water**
Mizu	Kōri mizu
MEE-ZOO	KO-REE MEE-ZOO

Mineral water

Mineraru uōtā

MEE-NE-Rah-ROO WO-Tah

AT THE BAR

Bartender

Bā ten dā

Bⓐⓗ Tⓔ̃N Dⓐⓗ

The wine list, please.

Wain risto o kudasai.

WⓘN BⓔⓔS-Tⓞ Ⓞ Kⓞⓞ-Dⓐⓗ-Sⓘ

Cocktail

Kakuteru

Kⓐⓗ-Kⓞⓞ-Tⓔ̃-Bⓞⓞ

With ice

Kōri-to

Kⓞ -Bⓔⓔ-Tⓞ

Straight

Sutoreito

STⓞ-Bⓐ-Tⓞ

With lemon

Remon mo

Bⓔ̃-MⓄ N Mⓞ

PHRASEMAKER

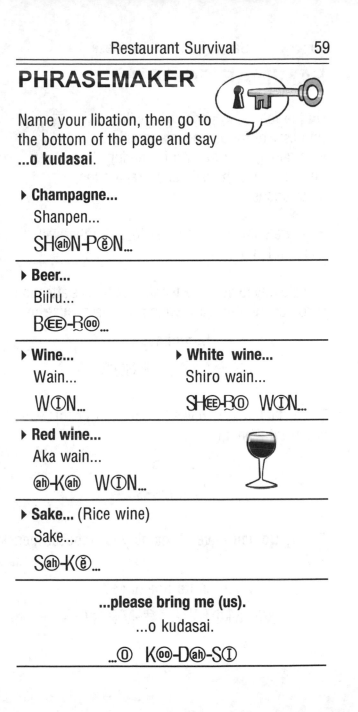

Name your libation, then go to the bottom of the page and say **...o kudasai**.

▸ **Champagne...**
Shanpen...
SH@N-P@N...

▸ **Beer...**
Biiru...
B@@-R@@...

▸ **Wine...**
Wain...
W@N...

▸ **White wine...**
Shiro wain...
SH@@-R@@ W@N...

▸ **Red wine...**
Aka wain...
@-K@ W@N...

▸ **Sake...** (Rice wine)
Sake...
S@-K@...

...please bring me (us).
...o kudasai.
...@ K@@-D@-S@

FAMILIAR FOODS

On the following pages you will
find lists of foods you are familiar
with, along with other information
such as basic utensils and preparation
instructions.

Here are some simple ways to order that will
come in handy.

A polite way to get a waiter's or waitress's attention
is to say **sumimasen**, which means **excuse me**:

Sumimasen

S⍟-M⍟-M⍟-S⍟N

To say **I'd like** (We'd like/Please bring) name what
you want then say:

...kudasai

...K⍟-D⍟-S⍟

To say **Do you have...?** name your request then
say:

...o motte imasu ka?

...⍟ M⍟T-T⍟ ⍟-M⍟S-K⍟

STARTERS

Appetizers

Zensai

ZĒN-SĪ

Bread	**Butter**
Pan	Batā
PⓐN	Bⓐ-Tⓐ

Cheese	**Fruit**
Chiizu	Kudamono
CHĒ-Zⓞⓞ	Kⓞⓞ-Dⓐ-Mⓞ-Nⓞ

Salad	**Soup**
Sarada	Sūpu
Sⓐ-Rⓐ-Dⓐ	Sⓞⓞ-Pⓞⓞ

Chicken soup

Chikin sūpu

CHĒ-KēN Sⓞⓞ-Pⓞⓞ

Vegetable soup

Yasai sūpu

Yⓐ-SĪ Sⓞⓞ-Pⓞⓞ

MEAT

Bacon

Bēkon

B⓮-K⓪N

Beef

Gyūniku

G⓮-⓪⓪-N⓮-K⓪⓪

Beef steak

Gyūniku sutēki

GY⓪⓪-N⓮-K⓪⓪ S⓪⓪-T⓮-K⓮

Ham

Hamu

Hⓐⓗ-M⓪⓪

Lamb

Ramu

RⓐⓗM

Pork

Butaniku

B⓪⓪-Tⓐⓗ-N⓮-K⓪⓪

Veal

Ko-ushi

K⓪-⓪⓪-SH⓮

POULTRY

Baked chicken

Bēkuto chikin

BĔ-KOO-TŌ CHEE-KEEN

Broiled chicken

Buroirudo chikin

BOO-ROY-ROO-DŌ CHEE-KEEN

Fried chicken

Furaido chikin

FOO-RĪ-DŌ CHEE-KEEN

Duck

Kamo

KAH-MŌ

Goose

Gachyō

GAH-CHŌ

Turkey

Shichimenchō

SHEE-CHEE-MĔN-CHŌ

SEAFOOD

Fish

Sakana

S@h-K@h-N@h

Lobster

Robusutā

R@-B@o-S@o-T@h

Oysters

Kaki

K@h-K@E

Salmon

Shake

SH@h-K@

Shrimp

Ebi

@-B@E

Trout

Masu

M@h-S@o

Tuna

Maguro

M@h-G@o-R@

OTHER ENTREES

Sandwich
Sandoicchi

S(ah)N-D(o)-(ee)-CH(ee)

Hot dog
Hotto doggu

H(o)T-T(o) D(o)G-G(oo)

Hamburger
Hambāgā

H(ah)M-B(ah)-G(ah)

French fries
Furench-furai

F(oo)-R(e)N-CH(ee) F(oo)-R(i)

Pasta
Pasuta

P(ah)-S(oo)-T(ah)

Pizza
Piza

P(ee)-Z(ah)

VEGETABLES

Carrots

Ninjin

NEEN-JEEN

Corn

Tōmorokoshi

TO-MO-RO-KO-SHEE

Mushrooms

Masshurūmu

MahSH-ROO-Moo

Onions

Tamanegi

Tah-Mah-Nē-GEE

Potato

Jagaimo

Jah-GI-MO

Rice (cooked)

Gohan

GO-HahN

Tomato

Tomato

TO-Mah-TO

FRUITS

Apple
Ringo
RⒺⒺN-GⓄ

Banana
Banana
BⓐⓗⒹ-Nⓐⓗ-Nⓐⓗ

Grapes
Budō
BⓄⓄ-DⓄ

Lemon
Remon
RⒺ̃-MⓄN

Orange
Orenji
Ⓞ-RⒺ̃N-JⒺⒺ

Strawberry
Ichigo
ⒺⒺ-CHⒺⒺ-GⓄ

Watermelon
Suika
SⓄⓄ-ⒺⒺ-Kⓐⓗ

DESSERT

Desserts

Dezāto

D**ĕ**-Z**ah**-T**O**

Apple pie

Apuru pai

ah-P**oo**-R**oo** P**I**

Cherry pie

Cherī pai

CH**ĕ**-R**EE** P**I**

Pastries

Pēsutorī

P**ĕ**-S**oo**-T**O**-R**EE**

Candy

Kyandē

KY**ah**N-D**A**

Ice cream

Aisu kurimu

I-SOO KOO-REE-MOO

Ice cream cone

Aisu kurīmu kon

I-SOO KOO-REE-MOO KON

Chocolate

Chokoreito

CHO-KO-RA-TO

Strawberry

Sutoroberi

STO-RO-Bĕ-REE

Vanilla

Banira

BAH-NEE-RAH

CONDIMENTS

Butter
Batā
Bⓐⓗ-Tⓐⓗ

Ketchup
Kechappu
Kⓔ-CHⓐⓗP-Pⓞⓞ

Mayonnaise
Mayonēzu
Mⓐⓗ-Yⓞ-Nⓔ-Zⓞⓞ

Mustard
Karashi
Kⓐⓗ-Rⓐⓗ-SHⓔⓔ

Salt
Shio
SHⓔⓔ-Ⓞ

Pepper
Koshō
Kⓞ-SHⓞ

Sugar
Satō
Sⓐⓗ-Tⓞ

Vinegar and oil
Su to oiru
Sⓞⓞ   Tⓞ   ⓞy-Rⓞⓞ

SETTINGS

A cup
Kappu
K(ah)P-P(oo)

A glass
Gurasu
G(oo)-R(ah)-S(oo)

A spoon
Supūn
S(oo)-P(oo)N

A fork
Fōku
F(o)-K(oo)

A knife
Naifu
N(i)-F(oo)

A plate
Sara
S(ah)-R(ah)

A napkin
Oshibori
(o)-SH(ee)-B(o)-R(ee)

HOW DO YOU WANT IT COOKED?

Baked

Bēkuto

B(A)-K(oo)-T(O)

Broiled

Buroirudo

B(oo)-R(oy)-R(oo)-D(O)

Steamed

Mushita

M(oo)-SH(EE)-T(ah)

Fried

Ageta

(ah)-G(ĕ)-T(ah)

Rare

Rea no

R(ĕ)-(ah) N(O)

Medium

Midiamu no

M(EE)-D(EE)-(ah)-M(oo) N(O)

Well done

Yoku yaita

Y(O)-K(oo) Y(I)-T(ah)

PROBLEMS

I didn't order this.

Kore o chūmon shimasen deshita.

KO-Rē O CHoo-MON
SHEE-Mah-SēN DēSH-Tah

Is the bill correct?

Okanjyō wa tadashii desu ka?

O-Kahn-JO Wah Tah-Dah-SHEE
DēS-Kah

May I change this?

Kaete itadake masu ka?

Kah-ē-Tē EE-Tah-Dah-Kē Mahs-Kah

PRAISE

Thank you for the delicious meal.

Gochisō sama deshita.

GO-CHEE-SO Sah-Mah DēSH-Tah

GETTING AROUND

Getting around in a foreign country can be an adventure in itself! Taxi and bus drivers do not always speak English, so it is essential to be able to give simple directions. The words and phrases in this chapter will help you get where you're going. Fortunately, Japan's public transportation system is one of the best in the world.

- Taxis are always metered.

- Have the address you want to go to written in Japanese.

- Trains are used frequently by visitors to Japan. Arrive early to allow time for ticket purchasing and checking in and remember, trains leave on time!

- Check with your travel agent about special rail passes such as the Japan Rail Pass that allow unlimited travel within a set period of time.

- It is not a good idea to take the subway or local trains during rush hours on weekdays when they are very crowded.

- Important signs are usually posted in English.

KEY WORDS

Airport
Kūkō

K⓪⓪-K⓪

Bus
Basu

Bⓐ-S⓪⓪

Car
Kuruma

K⓪⓪-R⓪⓪-Mⓐ

Car rental agency
Rentakāya

RⓔN-Tⓐ-Kⓐ-Yⓐ

Subway station
Chikatetsu no eki

CHⓔⓔ-Kⓐ-TⓔT-S⓪⓪ N⓪ ⓔ-Kⓔⓔ

Taxi stand
Takushī noriba

TⓐK-SHⓔⓔ N⓪-Rⓔⓔ-Bⓐ

Train station
Densha no eki

DⓔN-SHⓐ N⓪ ⓔ-Kⓔⓔ

AIR TRAVEL

Ticket

Kippu

K(EE)P-P(oo)

Where is the ticket window?

Kippu uriba wa doko desu ka?

K(EE)P-P(oo) (oo)-R(EE)-B(ah)

W(ah) D(O)-K(O) D(ĕ)S-K(ah)

How much are the tickets?

Kippu wa ikura desu ka?

K(EE)P-P(oo) W(ah)

(EE)-K(oo)-R(ah) D(ĕ)S-K(ah)

I'd like one ticket.

Kippu o ichimai kudasai.

K(EE)P-P(oo) (O) (EE)-CH(EE)-M(I)

K(oo)-D(ah)-S(I)

I'd like two tickets.

Kippu o nimai kudasai.

K(EE)P-P(oo) (O) N(EE)-M(I)

PHRASEMAKER

▶ **No smoking section...**

Kinen seki...

K⒠N-⒤N S⒤-K⒠...

▶ **A window seat..**

Mado giwa...

M⒜-D⒪ G⒠-W⒜...

▶ **An aisle seat...**

Tsūro gawa...

TS⒪⒪-R⒪ G⒜-W⒜...

▶ **An exit row..**

Iriguchi no chikaku...

⒠-R⒠-G⒪⒪-CH⒠ N⒪ CH⒠-K⒜-K⒪⒪...

...I would like.

...o kudasai

...⒪ K⒪⒪-D⒜-S⒤

BY BUS

Bus

Basu

B⒜-S⒪⒪

Where is the bus stop?

Basu noriba wa doko desu ka?

B⒜-S⒪⒪ N⒪-R⒠⒠-B⒜ W⒜
D⒪-K⒪ D⒠S-K⒜

Do you go to…?

…ni ikimasu ka?

…N⒠ ⒠-K⒠-M⒜S-K⒜

Name your destination first then **…ni ikimasu ka.**

What is the fare?

Unchin wa ikura desu ka?

⒪⒪N-CH⒠⒠N W⒜
⒠-K⒪⒪-R⒜ D⒠S-K⒜

Do I need exact change?

Kozeni no yōi ga hitsuyō deska?

K⒪-Z⒠-N⒠ N⒪ Y⒪-⒠
G⒜ H⒠⒠T-S⒪⒪-Y⒪ D⒠S-K⒜

PHRASEMAKER

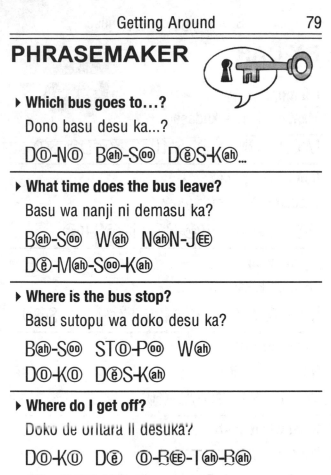

▶ **Which bus goes to…?**

Dono basu desu ka...?

DO-NO Bah-Soo DēS-Kah...

▶ **What time does the bus leave?**

Basu wa nanji ni demasu ka?

Bah-Soo Wah Nah N-JEE
Dē-Mah-Soo-Kah

▶ **Where is the bus stop?**

Basu sutopu wa doko desu ka?

Bah-Soo STO-Poo Wah
DO-KO DēS-Kah

▶ **Where do I get off?**

Doko de oritara ii desuka?

DO-KO Dē O-REE-Iah-Rah
EE DēS-Kah

BY CAR

Fill it up.

Mantan ni shite kudasai.

M@N-T@N N© SHT© K⊚-D@-S①

Can you help me?

Tasuke te kure masu ka?

T@S-K©-T© K⊚-R© M@S-K@

My car won't start.

Enjin ga kakarima sen.

©N-J©N G@ K@-K@-R©-M@ S©N

Can you fix it?

Nao se masu ka?

N@-① S© M@S-K@

What will it cost?

Ikura kakari masu ka?

©-K⊚-R@ K@-K@-R© M@S-K@

How long will it take?

Do no kurai kakari masu ka?

D① N① K⊚-R①
K@-K@-R© M@S-K@

PHRASEMAKER

▸ **The battery**

Batterī o...

B⒜T-T⒠-R⒠⒠ ⓞ...

▸ **The brakes**

Bureiki o..

B⒪⒪-R⒜-K⒠⒠ ⓞ...

▸ **The oil**

Oiru o...

ⓞ-⒠⒠-R⒪⒪ ⓞ...

▸ **The tires**

Taiya o...

T⒤-⒠⒠-Y⒜⒣ ⓞ...

▸ **The water**

Mizu o...

M⒠⒠-Z⒪⒪ ⓞ...

...please check.

...chekku shi te kudasai.

...CH⒠K-K⒪⒪ SHT⒠ K⒪⒪-D⒜⒣-S⒤

SUBWAYS AND TRAINS

Where is the subway station?

Chikatetsu no eki wa doko desu-ka?

CHEE-Kah-TēT-Soo NO ē-KEE Wah
DO-KO DēS-Kah

Where is the train station?

Eki-wa doko des-ka?

ē-KEE Wah DO-KO DēS-Kah

A one-way ticket, please.

Katamichi kippu o kudasai.

Kah-Tah-MEE-CHEE KEEP-Poo
O Koo-Dah-SI

A round-trip ticket.

Ofuku kippu.

O-Foo-Koo KEEP-Poo

First class.

Fāsuto kurasu.

Fah-Soo-TO Koo-Rah-Soo

Second class.

Sekando kurasu.

Sē-Kah N-DO Koo-Rah-Soo

Which train do I take to go to...

...ni iku densha wa dochira desu ka?

...NEE EE-KOO DĔN-SHah Wah DO-CHEE-Rah DĔS-Kah

Name the destination first!

What is the fare?

Unchin wa ikura desu ka?

OON-CHEEN Wah EE-KOO-Rah DĔS-Kah

Is this seat taken? (May I sit down?)

Suwatte mo ii desu ka?

SOO-WahT-TĔ MO EE DĔS-Kah

Do I have to change trains?

Norikae ga hitsuyō desu ka?

NO-REE-Kah-Ĕ Gah HEET-SOO-YO DĔS-Kah

Does this train stop at...

Kono densha ga...de tomarimasu ka?

KO-NO DĔN-SHah Gah... DĔ TO-Mah-REE-MahS-Kah

BY TAXI

Can you call a taxi for me?

Takushī o yonde kuremasu-ka?

T@K-SH㉿ ⓞ Y◉N-Dẽ
K⑩-Rẽ-M@S-K@

Are you available?

Ī desu ka?

㉿   Dẽ S-K@

I want to go to…

…ni ikitai desu.

…N㉿   ㉿-K㉿-T① Dẽ S

Name your destination first!

Stop here, please.

Koko de tomete kudasai.

K◉-K◉   Dẽ   T◉-Mẽ-Tẽ   K⑩-D@-S①

Please wait.

Chotto matte kudasai.

CH◉T-T◉   M@T-Tẽ   K⑩-D@-S①

How much do I owe?

Ikura desu ka?

㉿-K⑩-R@   Dẽ S-K@

PHRASEMAKER

In English we say **Please go to the airport**. In Japanese we say **The airport...please go to (it)**.

▶ **The hotel...**
Hoteru...

HO-Te-Roo...

▶ **To this address....**
Kono jūsho...

KO-NO JOO-SHO...

▶ **To the airport...**
Kū-kō...

KOO-KO...

▶ **The subway station...**
Chikatetsu...

CHEE-Kah-Tee T-Soo...

▶ **The hospital...**
Byōin...

BEE-O-EEN...

...please go to.

...ni itte kudasai.

...NEE EET-Te KOO-Dah-SI

SHOPPING

Whether you plan a major shopping spree or just need to purchase some basic necessities, the following information is useful.

- The Ginza is a shopping area in Tokyo known around the world.

- Mingei stores provide tourists with beautiful crafts from Japan. You can find hand-made dolls, pottery, and bamboo baskets.

- Sunday is the busiest shopping day of the week. Be sure to carry your passport with you for tax-free shopping.

- There are local shops for everyday needs, as well as large department stores and shopping centers. Most stores are open until 7:00 PM.

- Look for "Tax Free" signs, which will tell you which purchases qualify.

- When purchasing clothing, it is important to note that sizing in Japan is different from Western sizing.

- Bargaining is not common in the Japanese shopping experience.

KEY WORDS

Credit card

Kurejitto kādo

Koo-Rē-JeeT-To Kah-Do

Money

Okane

o-Kah-Nē

Receipt

Reshīto

Rē-SHee-To

Sale

Hanbai

HahN-Bi

Store

Mise

Mee-Sē

Travelers' checks

Toraberā chekku

To-Rah-Bē-Rah CHēK-Koo

USEFUL PHRASES

Do you sell…?

…o utteimasuka?

…Ⓞ ⓞⓞT-Tⓔ ⒺⒺ-MⓐⓗS-Kⓐⓗ

Name the item first then say **…o utteimasuka?**

Do you have…?

…ga arimasuka?

…Gⓐⓗ ⓐⓗ-ⓇⒺⒺ-MⓐⓗS-Kⓐⓗ

Name the item first then say **…ga arimasuka?**

I want to buy…

…o kaitai desu

…Ⓞ KⒾ-TⒾ Dⓔ̃S

Name the item first then say **…o kaitai desu.**

How much?

Ikura desu ka?

ⒺⒺ-Kⓞⓞ-Ⓡⓐⓗ Dⓔ̃S-Kⓐⓗ

When are the shops open?

Mise wa nanji ni akimasuka?

MⒺⒺ-Sⓔ̃ Wⓐⓗ NⓐⓗN-JⒺⒺ NⒺⒺ
ⓐⓗ-KⒺⒺ-MⓐⓗS-Kⓐⓗ

No, thank you.

Kekko desu.

KⒺK-KⓄ   DⒺS

I'm just looking.

Miru dake desu.

MⒺⒺ-RⓄⓄ   DⒶⒽ-KⒺⒺ   DⒺS

It's very expensive.

Takasugiru.

TⒶⒽ-KⒶⒽ-SⓄⓄ-GⒺⒺ-RⓄⓄ

Can't you give me a discount?

Benkyō dekimasu ka?

BⒺN-KYⓄ   DⒺ-KⒺⒺ-MⒶⒽS-KⒶⒽ

I'll take it.

Kore ni kimemasu.

KⓄ-RⒺ   NⒺⒺ   KⒺⒺ-MⒺ-MⒶⒽS

I'd like a receipt, please.

Reshīto o negai shimasu.

RⒺ-SHⒺⒺ-TⓄ   Ⓞ-NⒺ-GⒾ
SHⒺⒺ-MⒶⒽS

I want to return this.

Kore o kaeshitai no desu ga.

KⓄ-RⒺ   Ⓞ   KⒶⒽ-Ⓔ-SHⒺⒺ-TⒾ
NⓄ   DⒺS-GⒶⒽ

SHOPS AND SERVICES

To say I'm looking for...a bank, a florist, etc., name the establishment then say **...wa doko desu ka**. (W@h D©-K© D®S-K@h)

Bakery	**Florist**
Panya	Hanaya
P@N-Y@h	H@h-N@h-Y@h

Bank	**Hair salon**
Ginkō	Heā saron
G®N-K©	H®-@h S@h-R©N

Barber shop	**Jewelry store**
Tokoya	Hōseki ten
T©-K©-Y@h	H© -S®-K® T®N

Bookstore	**News stand**
Honya	Shinbun uriba
H©N-Y@h	SH®N-B©©N ©©-R®-B@h

Camera shop

Kamera ya

K@h-M®-B@h Y@h

Pharmacy

Yakkyoku

Y@hK-KY©-K©©

SHOPPING LIST

On the following pages you will find some common items you may need to purchase on your trip. To ask a clerk if a particular item is available, name the item first, then say **...ga irimasu ka.**
(G**ah** **EE**-**R****EE**-M**ah**S-K**ah**)

Aspirin
Asupirin

ahS-P**EE**-R**EE**N

Cigarettes
Tabako

T**ah**-B**ah**-K**O**

Deodorant
Deodoranto

D**A**-**O**-D**O**-R**ah**N-T**O**

Dress
Doresu

D**O**-R**ē**S

Film
Fuirumu

F**oo**-**EE**-R**oo**-M**oo**

Pantyhose

Pantī stokking

P@N-T㏄ ST⦿K-K㏄N-G⦿

Perfume

Kōsui

K⦿-S⦿-㏄

Razor blades

Kamisori no ha

K@-M㏄-S⦿-B㏄ N⦿ H@

Shampoo

Shanpū

SH@N-P⦿

Shaving cream

Shēbingu kurīmu

SH㋓-B㏄N-G⦿ K⦿-B㏄-M⦿

Shirt

Shatsu

SH@T-S⦿

Soap

Sekken

S㋓K-K㋓N

Sunglasses

San-guras

SaN-Goo-RahS

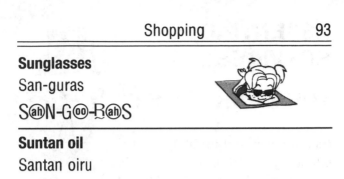

Suntan oil

Santan oiru

SaN-TaN oy-Roo

Toothbrushes

Ha burashi

Hah Boo-RahSH

Toothpaste

Ha migakiko

Hah MEE-Gah-KEE-KO

Water (bottled)

In ryosui

EEN REE-O-Soo-EE

Water (mineral)

Mineraru wota

MEE-Ne-Rah-Roo WO-Tah

ESSENTIAL SERVICES

THE BANK

As a traveler in a foreign country your primary contact with banks will be to exchange money.

- The unit of currency in Japan is the **yen.**

- Exchange rates fluctuate daily as they are dependent on the money market.

- Have your passport handy when changing money.

- Generally, you will receive a better rate of exchange at a bank than at an exchange office or airport.

- Current exchange rates are posted in banks and published daily in city newspapers.

- Cash, credit cards, and traveler's checks are accepted; however, personal checks are not usually accepted.

KEY WORDS

Bank

Ginkō

GEEN-KO

Exchange office

Ryōgaejo

REE-O-Gah-e-JO

Money

Okane

O-Kah-Ne

Money order

Yūbin kawase

YOO-BEEN Kah-Wah-Se

Traveler's checks

Toraberā chekku

TO-Rah-Be-Rah CHeK-Koo

Currencies

Tsuka

TSoo-Kah

USEFUL PHRASES

Where is the bank?

Ginkō-wa doko desu-ka?

GⒺⒺN-KⓄ Wⓐⓗ DⓄ-KⓄ DⓔⓢS-Kⓐⓗ

What time does the bank open?

Ginkō-wa nanji ni akimasu ka?

GⒺⒺN-KⓄ Wⓐⓗ NⓐⓗN-JⒺⒺ NⒺⒺ
ⓐⓗ-KⒺⒺ-MⓐⓗS-Kⓐⓗ

Where is the exchange office?

Ryōgaejo wa doko desu ka?

RⒺⒺ-Ⓞ-Gⓐⓗ-ⓔ-JⓄ
Wⓐⓗ DⓄ-KⓄ DⓔⓢS-Kⓐⓗ

What time does the exchange office open?

Ryōgaejo wa nanji ni akimasuka?

RⒺⒺ-Ⓞ-Gⓐⓗ-ⓔ-JⓄ Wⓐⓗ NⓐⓗN-JⒺⒺ
NⒺⒺ ⓐⓗ-KⒺⒺ-MⓐⓗS-Kⓐⓗ

Can I change dollars here?

Koko de doru o kaeraremasuka?

KⓄ-KⓄ Dⓔ DⓄ-Rⓞⓞ Ⓞ
Kⓐⓗ-ⓔ Rⓐⓗ-Rⓔ MⓐⓗS-Kⓐⓗ

Can you change this?

Kore o kaeraremasuka?

K◯-Bĕ̃ ◯ K⒜-ĕ̃ B⒜-Bĕ̃ M⒜S-K⒜

What is the exchange rate?

Kawase rēto wa ikura desu ka?

K⒜-W⒜-Sĕ̃ Bē-T◯ W⒜
Ⓔ-K⓪-B⒜ Dĕ̃S-K⒜

I would like large bills.

Kōgaku no osatsu de onegai shimasu.

K◯-G⒜-K⓪ N◯ ◯-S⒜T-S⓪ Dĕ̃
◯-Nĕ̃-G① SHⒺ-M⒜S

I would like small bills.

Osatsu de onegai shimasu.

◯-S⒜T-S⓪ Dĕ̃
◯-Nĕ̃-G① SHⒺ-M⒜S

Do you have an ATM?

Ei Tē Emu ga arimasu ka?

Ⓐ Tē ĕ-M⓪ G⒜
⒜-BⒺ-M⒜S-K⒜

POST OFFICE

If you are planning on sending
letters and postcards, be sure
to send them early so that you
don't arrive home before they do.

KEY WORDS

Airmail
Kōkūbin

KO-KOO-BEEN

Letter
Tegami

Te-Gah-MEE

Post office
Yūbin kyoku

YOO-BEEN KYO-Koo

Postcard
Hagaki

Hah-Gah-KEE

Stamp
Kitte

KEET-Te

USEFUL PHRASES

Where is the post office?

Yūbin kyoku wa doko desu ka?

YOO-BEEN KYO-KOO WAH
DO-KO DES-Kah

Pronounce **ky** like the **c** in **cu**te.

What time does the post office open?

Yūbin kyoku wa nanji ni akimasuka?

YOO-BEEN KYO-KOO WAH
NahN-JEE NEE ah-KEE-MahS-Kah

I need stamps.

Kitte ga irimasu.

KEET-Tĕ Gah EE-REE-MahS

I need a pen.

Pen ga irimasu.

PĕN Gah EE-REE-MahS

How much postage to...

...muke no tegami wa ikura desu ka?

MOO-Kĕ NO Tĕ-Gah-MEE WAH
EE-KOO-Rah DES-Kah

Name postage destination first.

TELEPHONE

Placing phone calls in a foreign
country can be a test of will and
stamina! Besides the obvious language
barriers, service can vary greatly from one
town to the next.

- If you have a choice, do not call from your
  hotel room. Service charges can add a
  hefty amount to your bill. If you use your
  hotel for long distance or international
  calls, use a calling card. This will cost
  you less than hotel charges; however, a
  fee may still be charged.

- You can purchase prepaid telephone cards
  from vending machines, convenience
  stores, and at train stations.

- Credit card and direct international calls
  can be made from telephones with an
  International and Domestic Telephone
  sign. These phones can be found at
  airports and hotels. Keep in mind that
  rates change often and these type of
  phones are not readily available.

KEY WORDS

Information
Jōhō

JⓄ-HⓄ

Long distance
Chōkyori denwa

CHⓄ-KYⓄ-Rᴇᴇ　DⓔN-Wₐₕ

Operator
Kōkanshu

KⓄ-KₐₕN-SHₒₒ

Phone book
Denwachyō

DⓔN-Wₐₕ-CHⓄ

Telephone
Denwa

DⓔN-Wₐₕ

USEFUL PHRASES

Where is the telephone?

Denwa-wa doko desu ka?

DĕN-W@h W@h DO-KO DĕS-K@h

Where is the public telephone?

Kō-shū denwa wa doko desu ka?

KO-SHoo DĕN-W@h
W@h DO-KO DĕS-K@h

May I use your telephone?

Denwa o tsukatte mo ii desu ka?

DĕN-W@h O TSoo-K@hT-Tĕ MO
EE DĕS-K@h

Information, please.

Denwa annai onegaishimasu.

DĕN-W@h @hN-NI O-Nĕ-GI
SHEE-M@hS

Hello

Moshi moshi

MO-SHEE MO-SHEE

I want to call this number...

Koko ni kaketai no desu ka...

KO-KO NEE K@-KĕTI

NO DĕS-K@...

SIGHTSEEING AND ENTERTAINMENT

In most cities and towns in Japan, you will find tourist information offices. Here you can usually obtain brochures, maps, historical information, bus and train schedules.

CITIES IN JAPAN

Tōkyo
TO-KYO

Kyoto
KYO-TO

Nagano
N@h-G@h-NO

Nagasaki
N@h-G@h-S@h-KEE

Osaka
O-S@h-K@h

Kamakura
K@h-M@h-K@o-R@h

Yokohama
YO-KO-H@h-M@h

Yokosuka
YO-KOoS-K@h

KEY WORDS

Admission

Nyūjōryō

NY⦿-J◍-R⦿-◍

Map

Chizu

CH⦿-Z⦿

Reservation

Yoyaku

Y◍-Y⦿-K⦿

Ticket

Kippu

K⦿P-P⦿

Tour

Tsuā

TS⦿-⦿

Tour guide

Tsuā gaido

TS⦿-⦿ G◍-D◍

USEFUL PHRASES

Where is the tourist office?

Ryokōsha annaijo wa doko desu ka?

REE-O-KO-SHah ahN-NI-JO
Wah DO-KO DeS-Kah

Where do I buy a ticket?

Kippu no uriba wa doko desu ka?

KEEP-Poo NO oo-REE-Bah
Wah DO-KO DeS-Kah

How much does the tour cost?

Kankō ryokō wa ikura desu ka?

Kah N-KO REE-O-KO Wah
EE-Koo-Bah DeS-Kah

How long does the tour take?

Nanji kan gurai kakarimasu ka?

NahN-JEE KahN Goo-RI
Kah-Kah-REE-MahS-Kah

Does the guide speak English?

Gaido-san wa eigo o hanashimasuka?

GI-DO SahN Wah A-GO O
Hah-Nah-SHEE-MahS-Kah

Are children free?

Kodomo wa tada desu ka?

KO-DO-MO Wah
Tah-Dah DeS-Kah

What time does the show start?

Shō wa itsu hajimarimasu ka?

SHO   Wah   EET-Soo
Hah-JEE-Mah-REE   MahS-Kah

Do I need reservations?

Yoyaku ga hitsuyō desu ka?

YO-Yah-Koo Gah
HEET-Soo-YO   DeS-Kah

Where is a place to go dancing?

Dansu suru tokoro wa doko desu ka?

DahN-Soo Soo-Roo TO-KO-RO Wah
DO-KO DeS-Kah

Is there a minimum cover charge?

Teburu chājiga arimasuka?

Te-Boo-Roo CHah-JEE-Gah
ah-REE-MahS-Kah

PHRASEMAKER

Name what you are looking for, then go to the bottom of the page and say **...ikimasen ka?**

▶ **To a theatre...**

Shiāta ni...

SH㋐-㋐-T㋐ N㋐...

▶ **To dinner...**

Kōnsato ni...

K㋔N-S㋐-T㋔ N㋐...

▶ **To dinner...**

Yushoku ni...

Y㋿-SH㋔-K㋿ N㋐

▶ **To a movie...**

Eiga ni...

Ⓐ-G㋐ N㋐...

...may I invite you?

...ikimasen ka?

㋐-K㋐-M㋐-S㋑N K㋐

PHRASEMAKER

▶ **A golf course...**

Goruhu kōsu wa...

GO-ROO-HOO KO-SOO Wah...

▶ **A health club...**

Herusu kurabu wa...

Hĕ-ROO-SOO KOO-Rah-BOO Wah...

▶ **A swimming pool...**

Suimingu pūru wa...

SOO-EE-MEEN-GOO POO-ROO Wah...

▶ **A tennis court...**

Tenisu koto wa...

Tĕ-NEE-SOO KO-TO Wah...

...where can I find?

...doko desu ka?

...DO-KO DĕS-Kah

HEALTH

Hopefully you will not need medical attention on your trip. If you do, it is important to communicate basic information regarding your condition.

- Check with your insurance company before leaving home to find out if you are covered in a foreign country. You may want to purchase traveler's insurance before leaving home.

- If you take prescription medicine, carry your prescription with you. Have your prescriptions translated before you leave home.

- Take a small first-aid kit with you.

- Hospitals in Japan offer a high standard of treatment should you experience a health problem during your visit.

- Your embassy or consulate should be able to assist you in finding health care.

KEY WORDS

Ambulance

Kyūkyūsha

KY(oo)-KY(oo)-SH(ah)

Dentist

Haisha

H(I)-SH(ah)

Doctor

Isha

(EE)-SH(ah)

Emergency

Kinkyū

K(EE)N-KY(oo)

Hospital

Byōin

B(EE)-(O)-(EE)N

Prescription

Shohōsen

SH(O)-H(O)-S(ĕ)N

USEFUL PHRASES

I am sick.

Byōki desu.

BEE-O-KEE DёS

I need a doctor.

Isha ga hitsuyō desu.

EE-SHah Gah HEET-Soo-YO DёS

It's an emergency!

Kinkyū desu!

KEEN-KYoo DёS

Where is the nearest hospital?

Ichiban chikai byōin wa doko desu ka?

EE-CHEE-BahN CHEE-KI

BEE-O-EEN Wah DO-KO DёS-Kah

Call an ambulance!

Kyūkyūsha o yonde!

KYoo-KYoo-SHah O YON-Dё

Pronounce **ky** like the c in **cu**te.

Call a doctor!

Isha o yonde!

EE-SHah O YON-Dё

I'm allergic to…

…ni arerugī desu.

…NEE ah-REE-ROO-GEE DēS

Name what you're allergic to first.

I'm pregnant.

Ninshin shite imas.

NEEN-SHEEN SHEE-Tē EE-MahS

I'm diabetic.

Tōnyōbyō desu.

TO-NYO-BEE-O DēS

I have a heart condition.

Shinzōbyō.

SHEEN-ZO-BEE-O

I have high blood pressure.

Kōketsuatsu des.

KO-KēT-SOO-ahT-SOO DēS

I have low blood pressure.

Tēketsuatsu desu.

Tē-KēT-SOO-ahT-SOO DēS

PHRASEMAKER

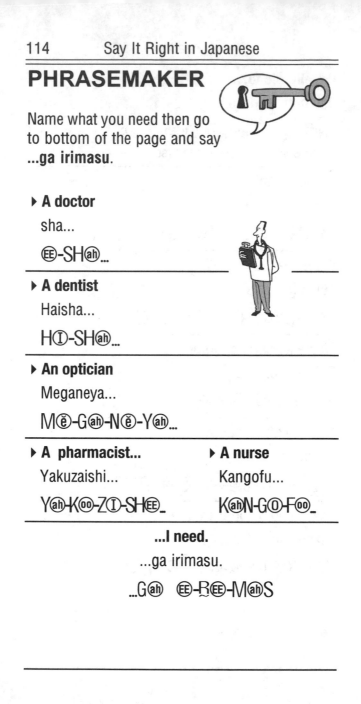

Name what you need then go
to bottom of the page and say
...ga irimasu.

▶ **A doctor**

sha...

Ⓔ-SHⓐ...

▶ **A dentist**

Haisha...

HⒾ-SHⓐ...

▶ **An optician**

Meganeya...

MⒺ-Gⓐ-NⒺ-Yⓐ...

▶ **A pharmacist...**

Yakuzaishi...

Yⓐ-Kⓞⓞ-ZⒾ-SHⒺ...

▶ **A nurse**

Kangofu...

Kⓐ-N-GⓄ-Fⓞⓞ...

...I need.

...ga irimasu.

...Gⓐ Ⓔ-RⒺ-Mⓐ-S

PHRASEMAKER
(AT THE PHARMACY)

▸ **Aspirin**

Asupirin...

@S-P©-R©N

▸ **Band-Aids**

Bando eido...

B@N-D© @-D©

▸ **Cough medicine**

Seki shiroppu...

S©-K© SH©-R©P-P©

▸ **Ear drops**

Mimigusuri...

M©-M©-G©-S©-D©

▸ **Eyedrops?**

Megusuri...

M©-G©-S©-R©

▸ **Medicine**

Kusuri...

K©-S©-R©

...I need.

...ga irimasu.

...G@ ©-R©-M@S

BUSINESS TRAVEL

It is important to show appreciation and interest in another person's language and culture, particularly when doing business. A few well-pronounced phrases can make a great impression.

- Exchanging business cards is very important, so be sure to bring a good supply with you.

- Present your business card with the Japanese side facing up, holding it in both hands after a bow.

- When you receive a card, be sure to examine and remark on it and then place it in your card case.

- Writing on a business card or placing it in your pocket is considered disrespectful.

- Participating in the bowing custom shows interest in Japanese customs and is appreciated.

- Business dress is conservative. You will be asked to remove your shoes in temples and homes.

- Gift giving is also an important part of Japanese business. However, there are many rules to consider such as etiquette with regard to number, presentation, and timing.

KEY WORDS

Appointment
Yoyaku

YⓄ-Yⓐʰ-Kⓞⓞ

Business card
Meishi

Mⓐ-SHⒺⒺ

Meeting
Kaigi

KⒾ-GⒺⒺ

Marketing
Mākettingu

Mⓐʰ-Kⓔ̃T-TⒺⒺN-Gⓞⓞ

Office
Jimusho

JⒺⒺ-Mⓞⓞ-SHⓄ

Presentation
Purezentāsyon

Pⓞⓞ-Rⓔ̃-Zⓔ̃N-Tⓐʰ-SHⓄN

Telephone
Denwa

Dⓔ̃N-Wⓐʰ

USEFUL PHRASES

I have an appointment.

Yoyaku ga arimasu.

Y◎-Y@-K⑳ G@ @-R㋐-M@S

My name is…(your name)…Pleased to meet you.

…(your name)…desu Hajimemashite.

Dōzo yoroshiku.

(your name)…D㋑S

H@-J㋐-M㋑-M@SH-T㋑

D◎-Z◎ Y◎-R◎SH-K⑳

Here is my card.

Meishi o dōzo.

M④-SH㋐ ◎ D◎-Z◎

Exchanging business cards should be done in a slow manner. Hold your card with both hands with Japanese printing facing the recipient. Be sure to read carefully and remark on your counterpart's card and carefully place in a card carrying case.

Can we get an interpreter?

Tsūyakushya o onegaidekimasuka?

TS⑳-Y@-K⑳-SH@ ◎

◎-N㋑-G@   ㋐-D㋑-K㋐-M@S-K@

Can you write your address for me?

Adoresu o kaite kuremasu ka?

ⓐ-DⓄ-Rⓔ-Sⓞⓞ

Ⓞ K①-Tⓔ Kⓞⓞ-Rⓔ-Mⓐ-Sⓐ-Kⓐ

Can you write your phone number?

Denwa sangō o kaite kuremasu ka?

Dⓔ-N-Wⓐ Sⓐ-N-GⓄ

Ⓞ K①-Tⓔ Kⓞⓞ-Rⓔ-Mⓐ-Sⓐ-Kⓐ

This is my phone number.

Kore ga watashi no denwa bangō desu.

KⓄ-Rⓔ Gⓐ Wⓐ-Tⓐ-SHⓔⓔ NⓄ

Dⓔ-N-Wⓐ Bⓐ-N-GⓄ Dⓔ-S

His/Her name is...

Namae wa...desu.

Nⓐ-Mⓐ-ⓔ Wⓐ...Dⓔ-S

Thank you.

Arigatō.

ⓐ-Rⓔⓔ-Gⓐ-TⓄ

Goodbye. See you soon.

Sayōnara. Mata o aishima shō.

Sⓐ-YⓄ-Nⓐ-Rⓐ

Mⓐ-Tⓐ Ⓞ ①-SHⓔⓔ-Mⓐ SHⓄ

PHRASEMAKER

Name what you need, then go to the bottom of the next page and say **...ga irimasu.**

▸ **A computer...**

Konpyūtā...

KⓄN-PYⓄⓄ-Tⓐⓗ...

▸ **A copy machine...**

Kopī mashīn...

KⓄ-PⒺⒺ Mⓐⓗ-SHⒺⒺN...

▸ **A conference room...**

Kaigishitsu...

KⒾ-GⒺⒺ-SHⒺⒺT-SⓄⓄ...

▸ **A fax or fax machine...**

Fakkusu...

FⓐⓗK-KⓄⓄ-SⓄⓄ...

▸ **An interpreter......**

Tsūyakusha...

TSⓄⓄ-Yⓐⓗ-KⓄⓄ-SHⓐⓗ...

▸ **A lawyer...**

Bengoshi...

BⒺN-GⓄ-SHⒺⒺ...

▸ **A notary...**

Kōshōnin...

KO-SHO-NEEN...

▸ **A pen...**

Pen...

PEN...

▸ **Stamps...**

Kitte...

KEET-TE...

▸ **Stationery...**

Bunbōgu...

BOON-BO-GOO...

▸ **Typing paper...**

Taipuyōshi...

TI-POO-YO-SHEE...

...I need.

...ga irimasu

...Gah EE-REE-Mahs

GENERAL INFORMATION

Japan is covered by hills and mountains and enjoys distinctive seasonal changes. Summers can be very hot and humid.

SEASONS

Spring

haru

Hah-Roo

Summer

natsu

Naht-Soo

Autumn

aki

ah-Kee

Winter

fuyu

Foo-Yoo

THE DAYS

Monday
getsuyōbi

G⊚T-S⊚-Y⊙-B⊕

Tuesday
kayōbi

K⊚-Y⊙-B⊕

Wednesday
suiyōbi

S⊚-⊕-Y⊙-B⊕

Thursday
mokuyōbi

M⊙-K⊚-Y⊙-B⊕

Friday
kinyōbi

K⊕N-Y⊙-B⊕

Saturday
doyōbi

D⊙-Y⊙-B⊕

Sunday
nichiyōbi

N⊕-CH⊕-Y⊙-B⊕

THE MONTHS

January
ichigatsu
EE-CHEE-Gah-T-Soo

February
nigatsu
NEE-Gah-T-Soo

March
sangatsu
Sah-N-Gah-T-Soo

April
shigatsu
SHEE-Gah-T-Soo

May
gogatsu
GO-Gah-T-Soo

June
rokugatsu
RO-Koo-Gah-T-Soo

July
shichigatsu
SHEE-CHEE-Gah-T-Soo

August
hachigatsu
Hah-CHEE-Gah-T-Soo

September
kūgatsu
KOO-Gah-T-Soo

October
jūgatsu
JOO-Gah-T-Soo

November
jūichigatsu
JOO-EE-CHEE-Gah-T-Soo

December
jūnigatsu
JOO-NEE-Gah-T-Soo

COLORS

Black
Kuroi
K(oo)-R(O)-(EE)

White
Shiroi
SH(EE)-R(O)-(EE)

Blue
Aoi
(ah)-(O)-(EE)

Brown
Chairoi
CH(I)-R(O)-(EE)

Gray
Hai iro no
H(I) (EE)-R(O) N(O)

Gold
Kin no
K(EE)N N(O)

Orange
Orenji iro no
(O)-R(e)N-J(EE) (EE)-R(O) N(O)

Yellow
Kiiroi
K(EE)-R(O)-(EE)

Rod
Akai
(ah)-K(I)

Groon
Midori iro no
M(EE)-D(O)-R(EE) (EE)-R(O) N(O)

Pink
Momo iro no
M(O)-M(O) (EE)-R(O) N(O)

Purple
Murasaki iro no
M(oo)-R(ah)-S(ah)-K(EE) (EE)-R(O) N(O)

NUMBERS

0	**1**	**2**
zéro	ichi	ni
ZĒ-RO	EE-CHEE	NEE

3	**4**	**5**
san	shi/yon	go
SahN	SHEE/YON	GO

6	**7**	**8**
roku	shichi	hachi
RO-Koo	SHEE-CHEE	Hah-CHEE

9	**10**	**11**
kyū	jū	jū-ichi
KYoo	Joo	Joo-EE-CHEE

12	**13**	**14**
jū-ni	jū-san	jū-shi
Joo-NEE	Joo-SahN	Joo-SHEE

15	**16**
jū-go	jū-roku
Joo-GO	Joo-RO-Koo

17	**18**
jū-nana	jū-hachi
Joo-Nah-Nah	Joo-Hah-CHEE

19
ju-ku
J〇〇-K〇〇

20
ni-ju
N㋑-J〇〇

30
san-jū
S㋐N-J〇〇

40
shi-jū
SH㋑-J〇〇

50
go-ju
G〇-J〇〇

60
rokku-jū
R〇K-K〇〇 J〇〇

70
nana-jū
N㋐-N㋐-J〇〇

80
hachi-jū
H㋐-CH㋑ J〇〇

90
kyū-jū
KY〇〇-J〇〇

100
hyaku
H㋑-㋐-K〇〇

1000
sen
S㋑N

1,000,000
hyaku-man
H㋑-㋐-K〇〇-M㋐N

DICTIONARY

Each English word is followed by the Japanese word and then the EPLS pronunciation.

A

able (to be) ga dekimasu Gah DĒ-KĒE-Mah-S

above ueni ⓞⓞ-ē-NĒE

accident jiko JĒE-Kⓞ

address jūsho Jⓞⓞ-SHⓞ

admission fee nyūjōryō NYⓞⓞ-Jⓞ-Rēe-ⓞ

afraid kowagaru Kⓞ-Wah-Gah-Rⓞⓞ

after atode ah-Tⓞ-Dē

afternoon gogo Gⓞ-Gⓞ

airplane hikōki Hēe-Kⓞ-Kēe

airline kōkū Kⓞ-Kⓞⓞ

airmail kōkūbin Kⓞ-Kⓞⓞ-Bēen

airport kūkō Kⓞⓞ-Kⓞ

all zenbu Zēn-Bⓞⓞ

almost hotondo Hⓞ-Tⓞn-Dⓞ

---

alone hitori HEE-TO-REE

also momata MO-Mah-Tah

always itsumo EET-Soo-MO

ambulance kyūkyūsha KYoo-KYoo-SHah

America Amerika ah-MEĕ-REE-Kah

American America jin ah-MEĕ-REE-Kah JEEN

and to TO

another betsuno BEĕT-Soo-NO

appetizers zensaiv ZEĕN-SI

apple ringo REEN-GO

appointment yoyaku YO-Kah-Koo

April shigatsu SHEE-Gah-T-Soo

arrival tochaku TO-CHah-Koo

ashtray haizara HI-Zah-Rah

aspirin aspirin ahS-PEE-REEN

August hachigatsu Hah-CHEE-Gah-T-Soo

Australia Osutoraria O-STO-Rah-REE-ah

Australian Osutoraria jin

   O-STO-Rah-REE-ah JEEN

author sakka S(ah)K-K(ah)

automobile jidōsha J(EE)-D(O)-SH(ah)

Autumn / Fall (season) aki (ah)-K(EE)

awful hidoi H(EE)-D(O)-(EE)

B

baby akachan (ah)-K(ah)-CH(ah)N

babysitter komori K(O)-M(O)-R(EE)

bacon bēkon B(ě)-K(O)N

bad warui W(ah)-R(oo)-(EE)

baggage nimotsu N(EE)-M(O)T-S(oo)

baked bēkudo poteto B(ě)-K(oo)-D(O) P(O)-T(ě)-T(O)

bakery pan ya P(ah)N Y(ah)

banana banana B(ah)-N(ah)-N(ah)

Band-Aids bandoeido B(ah)N-D(O)-(A)-D(O)

bank ginkō G(EE)N-K(O)

barbershop tokoya T(O)-K(O)-Y(ah)

bath basu B(ah)-S(oo)

beach kaigan K(I)-G(ah)N

beautiful kireina K(EE)-R(A)-N(ah)

beauty salon biyō shitsu BEE-YO SHEET-SOO

bed beddo BED-DOO

beef bifu BEE-FOO

beer bīru BEE-ROO

bellman bōi BO-EE

belt beruto BE-ROO-TO

big ōkii O-KEE

black kuroi KOO-RO-EE

blanket mōfu MO-FOO

blue aoi ah-O-EE

boat bōto BO-TO

bookstore honya HON-Yah

bracelet buresuretto BOO-RE-SOO-RET-TO

bread pan PahN

breakfast asagohan ah-Sah-GO-HahN

broiled buroirudo BOO-ROy-ROO-DO

brother kyōdai KYO-DI

brown chairoi CHI-RO-EE

brush burashi BOO-Rah-SHEE

building biru BEE-Roo

bus basu Bah-Soo

bus stop basu noriba Bah-Soo NO-REE-Bah

business shigoto SHEE-GO-TO

butter batā Bah-Tah

buy (to) kau Kah-oo

C

cab takushī Tah-K-SHEE

call (to) telephone denwa suru

    DeN-Wah Soo-Roo

camera kamera Kah-Me-Rah

Canada Canada Kah-Nah-Dah

Canadian Canada jin Kah-Nah-Dah JEEN

candy kyandē KYahN-DA

car kuruma Koo-Roo-Mah

carrot ninjin NEEN-JEEN

celebration oiwai O-EE-WI

cereal shiriaru SHEE-REE-ah-Roo

chair isu EE-Soo

champagne shanpen SH@N-P@N

chango (to) kaeru K@-@-R@@

change (exact) kozeni K@-Z@-N@

cheap yasui Y@-S@@-@

check, please (restaurant bill)

kanjyō kudasai K@N-J@ K@@-D@-S@

chekku kudasai CH@K-K@@ K@@-D@-S@

cheers! kanpai! K@N-P@

cheese chiizu CH@-Z@@

chicken chikin CH@-K@N

child (your) kodomo K@-D@-M@

child (another's child) okoson @K@-S@N

China Chīgoku CH@-@-K@@

Chinese Chīgoku jin CH@-G@-K@@ J@N

chocolate chokolēto CH@-K@-L@-T@

church kyōkai K@-@-K@

cigar hamaki H@-M@-K@

cigarette tabako T@-B@-K@

city shi / toshi SH@ / T@-SH@

clean   kirei na   KEE-REe Nah

closed   shimatteiru   SHEE-Mah-T-Te-EE-Roo

clothes   yōfuku   YO-Foo-Koo

cocktails   kakuteru   Kah-Koo-Te-Roo

coffee   kōhī   KO-HEE

cold (temperature)   samui   Sah-Moo-EE

comb   kushi   Koo-SHEE

come (to)   kuru   Koo-Roo

company   kaisha   KI-SHah

computer   konpyūtā   KON-PYoo-Tah

concert   konsāto   KON-Sah-TO

condom   kondōmu   KON-DO-Moo

conference room   kaigishitsu

   KI-GEE-SHEET-Soo

congratulations   omedetō   O-Me-De-TO

copy machine   kopī   mashīn

   KO-PEE   Mah-SHEEN

corn   kōn   KON

cough syrup sekidome shiroppu

SĒ-KĒ-DO-MŌ SHĒ-ROP-Poo

cover charge kabā chāji Kah-Bah CHah-JĒ

crab kani Kah-NĒ

cream kurīmu-to Koo-RĒ-Moo TO

credit card kurejitto kādo

Koo-RĒ-JĒT-TO Kah-DO

cup kappu KahP-Poo

customs zeikan ZA-Kah N

D

dancing odotte O-DOT-Tē

date (calender) nichi NĒ-CHĒ

day hi HĒ

December jūnigatsu Joo NĒ-Gah T-Soo

delicious oishii O-Ē-SHĒ

dentist haisha HO-SHah

deodorant deodoranto DĒ-O-DO-Rah N-TO

department store depāto DĒ-Pah-TO

departure shuppatsu SHoo P-Pah T-Soo

dessert   dezāto   Dĕ-Zah-TO

diabetic   tōnyōbyō   TON-YO-BEE-YO

diarrhea   geri   Gĕ-REE

dictionary   jisho   JEE-SHO

dinner   yū shoku   YOO   SHO-KOO

dining room   shokudō   SHO-KOO-DO

directions   hōkō   HO-KO

dirty   kitanai   KEE-Tah-Nah-EE

discount   waribiki   Wah-REE-BEE-KEE

doctor   isha   EE-SHah

document   shorui   SHO-ROO-EE

dollar   doru   DO-ROO

down   shita ni   SHEE-Tah   NEE

downtown   hangagai   HahN-Gah-GĪ

dress   doresu   DO-Rĕ-SOO

dressing room   shichaku shitsu
   SHEE-CHah-KOO   SHEET-SOO

drink (to)   nomu   NO-MOO
   (nomimasu)   (NO-MEE-MahS)

drive (to)   unten suru   ⓄN-TⓔN SⓄⓄ-RⓄⓄ

  (unten shimas)   (ⓄN TⓔN SHⒺⒺ-Mⓐⓢ)

drugstore   doraggusutoa   DⓄ-RⓐⓗG-GⓄⓄ-STⓄ-ⓐⁿ

dry cleaner   doraikurīningu

  DⓄ-RⓄⒾ KⓄⓄ-RⒺⒺ-NⒺⒺN-GⓄⓄ

duck   kamo   Kⓐⓗ-MⓄ

E

ear   mimi   MⒺⒺ-MⒺⒺ

ear drops   mimi gusuri   MⒺⒺ-MⒺⒺ GⓄⓄ-SⓄⓄ-RⒺⒺ

early   hayaku   Hⓐⓗ-Yⓐⓗ-KⓄⓄ

east   higashi   HⒺⒺ-Gⓐⓗ-SHⒺⒺ

easy   yasashii   Yⓐⓗ-Sⓐⓗ-SHⒺⒺ

eat (to)   taberu   Tⓐⓗ Dⓔ-Rⓤ

egg   tamago   Tⓐⓗ-Mⓐⓗ-GⓄ

eggs (fried)   medama-yaki   Mⓔ-Dⓐⓗ-Mⓐⓗ Yⓐⓗ-KⒺⒺ

eggs (scrambled)   kaki tamago

  Kⓐⓗ-KⒺⒺ Tⓐⓗ-Mⓐⓗ-GⓄ

electricity   denki   Dⓔ̄N-KⒺⒺ

elevator   erebētā   ⓔ-Ꝛⓔ-Ꝛⓔ-Tⓐh

embassy   taishi kan   Tⓘ-SHⒺ Kⓐh N

emergency   kinkyū jitai   KⒺN-KYⓞⓞ Jⓔⓔ-Tⓘ

England   igirisu   ⒺⒺ-GⒺⒺ-ꝚⒺⒺ-Sⓞⓞ

English   igirisu jin   ⒺⒺ-GⒺⒺ-ꝚⒺⒺ-Sⓞⓞ JⒺⒺN

entrance   iriguchi   ⒺⒺ-ꝚⒺⒺ-Gⓞⓞ-CHⒺⒺ

envelope   fūtō   Fⓞⓞ-Tⓘ

evening   yūgata   Yⓞⓞ-Gⓐh-Tⓐh

everything   zenbu   Zⓔ N-Ꝛⓞⓞ

excellent   yūshūna   Yⓞⓞ-SHⓞⓞ-Nⓐh

excuse me   sumimasan   Sⓞⓞ-MⒺⒺ-Mⓐh-Sⓔ N

exit   deguchi   Dⓔ-Gⓞⓞ-CHⒺⒺ

expensive   takai   Tⓐh-Kⓘ

eye   me   MⒺⒺ

eyedrops   megusuri   MⒺⒺ-Gⓞⓞ-Sⓞⓞ-ꝚⒺⒺ

F

face   kao   Kⓐh-ⓞ

far   tōi   Tⓘ-ⒺⒺ

fare   ryōkyn   ꝚⒺⒺ-ⓘ-KⒺⒺN

fax fakkusu Fah-K-Koo-Soo

February nigatsu Nee-Gah-T-Soo

few (a little) sukoshi SKO-SHee

film (camera) firumu Fee-Roo-Moo

finger yubi Yoo-Bee

fire! kaji! Kah-Jee

first ichiban ee-CHee-Bah-N

fish sakana Sah-Kah-Nah

flight number bin mei Bee-N MI

florist (shop) hanaya Hah-Nah-Yah

flower hana Hah-Nah

foot ashi ah-SHee

fork fōku FO-Koo

french fries furench-furai
  Foo-Ree-N-CHee Foo-RI

Friday kin-yōbi Kee-N-YO-Bee

fried furaido Foo-RI-DO

fruit kudamono Koo-Dah-MO-NO

G

gas station   gasorin stando

  Gah-SO-REEN STah-N-DO

gasoline   gasorin   Gah-SO-REEN

gentleman   shinshi   SHEEN-SHEE

gift   okurimono   O-KOO-REE-MO-NO

glass (drinking)   gurasu   GOO-Rah-OO

glasses (eye)   megane   MĕĕG-Gah-Nĕĕ

gloves   tebukuro   Tĕĕ-BOO-KOO-RO

go   iku   EE-KOO

gold   kin   KEEN

golf   gorufu   GO-ROO-FOO

golf course   gorufu kōsu   GO-ROO-FOO KO-SOO

good   ii   EE

good-bye   sayōnara   Sah-YO-Nah-Rah

goose   gachyō   Gah-CHO

grapes   budō   BOO-DO

gray   gurē   GOO-Rĕĕ

green   midori iro no   MEE-DO-REE EE-RO NO

grocery store (supermarket) sūpā SOO-Pah

guide gaido GI-DO

H

hair kami Kah-MEE

hairbrush heā burashi HE-ah BOO-Rah-SHEE

haircut san patsu SahN Pah-TSOO

hair salon heā saron HE-ah Sah-RON

ham hamu Hah-MOO

hamburger hanbāgā HahN-Bah-Gah

hand te TE

happy ureshii OO-RE-SHEE

he kare wa Kah-RE Wah

head atama ah-Tah-Mah

headache zutsū ZOOT-SOO

health club herusu kurabu

HE-ROO-SOO KOO-Rah-BOO

heart shinzō SHEEN-ZO

heart attack shinzō mahi

SHEEN-ZO Mah-HEE

heater danbō D⃝ahN-B⃝O

hello (telephone) moshi moshi
  M⃝O-SH⃝EE M⃝O-SH⃝EE

help! tasukete! T⃝ahS-K⃝eh-T⃝eh

here koko K⃝O-K⃝O

holiday saijitsu S⃝I-J⃝EET-S⃝oo

hospital byōin B⃝EE-Y⃝O-⃝EEN

hot dog hotto doggu H⃝OT-T⃝O D⃝OG-G⃝oo

hotel hoteru H⃝O-T⃝eh-R⃝oo

hour jikan J⃝EE-K⃝ahN

how dō yatte D⃝O Y⃝ahT-T⃝eh

husband shujin SH⃝oo-J⃝EEN

I

I watakushi ga W⃝ah-T⃝ah-K⃝oo-SH⃝EE G⃝ah

ice kōri K⃝O-R⃝EE

ice cream aisu kurīmu ⃝I-S⃝oo K⃝oo-R⃝EE-M⃝oo

ill byōki B⃝EE-⃝O-K⃝EE

important jūyōna J⃝oo-Y⃝O-N⃝ah

information annai ⃝ahN-N⃝I

inn ryokan R(EE)-(O)-K(ah)N

interpreter tsūyakushya TS(oo)-Y(ah)-K(oo)-SH(ah)

J

jacket jaketto J(ah)-K(e)T-T(o)

jam jamu J(ah)-M(oo)

January ichigatsu (EE)-CH(EE)-G(ah)T-S(oo)

Japan Nihon N(EE)-H(O)N

Japanese Nihongo N(EE)-H(O)N-G(O)

jewelry store hosekiten H(O)-S(e)-K(EE)-T(e)N

juice jūsu J(oo)-S(oo)

July shichigatsu SH(EE)-CH(EE)-G(ah)T-S(oo)

June rokugatsu R(O)-K(oo)-G(ah)T-S(oo)

K

ketchup kechappu K(e)-CH(ah)P-P(oo)

key kagi K(ah)-G(EE)

kiss kisu K(EE)-S(oo)

knife naifu N(I)-F(oo)

L

ladies' restroom fujinyō toire

　FOO-JEEN-YO TO-EE-REe

lamb ramu Rah-M

large ōkii O-KEE

late osoi O-SO-EE

later ato de ah-TO Dee

laundry sentakumono SEN-Tah-K-oo-MO-NO

lawyer bengoshi BEN-GO-SHI

left (direction) hidari HEE-Dah-REE

leg ashi ah-SHEE

lemon remon REe-MON

less motto sukunaku MOT-TO SKoo-Nah-Koo

letter tegami TEe-Gah-MEE

lettuce retas REe-Tah'S

light denki DEN-KEE

like ga sukidesu Gah Soo-KEE-DeS

lip kuchibiru Koo-CHEE-BEE-Roo

lipstick kuchibeni Koo-CHEE-BEe-NEE

little (amount) sukoshi SK⊚-SHⒺ

live (reside) sumu S⊚⊚-M⊚⊚

lobster robusutā R⊚-B⊚⊚-S⊚⊚-T⊚

long (adj) nagai N⊚-G①

lost nakushimashita N⊚-K⊚⊚-SHⒺ-M⊚SH-T⊚

love (to) aisu ①-S⊚⊚

  (aishimasu) (①-SHⒺ-M⊚-S⊚⊚)

luck un ⊚⊚N

luggage nimotsu NⒺ-M⊚T-S⊚⊚

lunch hirugohan HⒺ-R⊚⊚-G⊚-H⊚N

M

maid mēdo M⊕-D⊚

mall yubin Y⊚⊚-BⒺN

makeup keshō K⊕-SH⊚

man otoko ⊚-T⊚-K⊚

manager manējā M⊚N-⊕-J⊚

map chizu CHⒺ-Z⊚⊚

March sangatsu S⊚N-G⊚T-S⊚⊚

market ichiba ⒺE-CHⒺ-B⊚

matches (light)   matchi   MⓐT-CHⒺ

May   gogatsu   GⓄ-GⓐT-Sⓞⓞ

mayonnaise   mayonēzu   Mⓐ-YⓄ-NⒶ-Zⓞⓞ

meal   shokuji   SHⓄ-Kⓞⓞ-JⒺ

meat   niku   NⒺ-Kⓞⓞ

medicine   kusuri   Kⓞⓞ-Sⓞⓞ-RⒺ

meeting   kaigi   KⒾ-GⒺ

mens' restroom   danshi yō no toire

　DⓐN-SHⒺ   YⓄ   NⓄ   TⓄ-Ⓔ-Rⓔ

menu   menū   MⓔN-Yⓞⓞ

message   messēji   MⓔS-Sⓔ-JⒺ

milk   miruku   MⒺ-Rⓞⓞ-Kⓞⓞ

mineral water   mineraru uōtā

　MⒺ-Nⓔ-Rⓐ-Rⓞⓞ   ⓞⓞ-Ⓞ-Tⓐ

Miss (add san to name)   SⓐN

mistake   gokai   GⓄ-KⒾ

Monday   getsuyōbi   GⓔT-Sⓞⓞ-YⓄ-BⒺ

money   okane   Ⓞ-Kⓐ-Nⓔ

month   gatsu   GⓔT-Sⓞⓞ

monument kinenhi KEE-NEN-HEE

more motto MOT-TO

morning asa ah-Sah

mother okāsan O-Kah-SahN

mountain yama Yah-Mah

movie theater eigakan A-Gah-KahN

Mr. (add san to name) SahN

Mrs. (add san to name) SahN

museum hakubutsukan Hah-Koo-Boo-TSoo-KahN

mushrooms masshurūmu MahSH-Boo-Moo

music ongaku ON-Gah-Koo

mustard karashi Kah-Bah-SHEE

N

name namae Nah-Mah-e

napkin oshibori O-SHEE-BO-BEE

near chikai CHEE-KI

neck kubi Koo-BEE

need (to) iru / hitsuyō da
    EE-Boo / HEET-Soo-YO Dah

news stand   shinbun uriba

  SHⒺN-BⓄN ⓄⓄ-RⒺE-Bⓐh

next time   jikai   JⒺE-KⒾ

night   yoru   YⓄ-RⓄⓄ

nightclub   naito kurabu   NⒾ-TⓄ KⓄⓄ-Rⓐh-BⓄⓄ

no   iie   ⒺE-ⓔ̆

no smoking   kin-en   KⒺN-ⓔ̆N

noon   hiru   HⒺE-RⓄⓄ

north   kita   KⒺE-Tⓐh

notary   kōshōnin   KⓄ-SHⓄ-NⒺEN

November   jūichigatsu   JⓄⓄ-ⒺE-CHⒺE-GⓐhT-SⓄⓄ

nurse (a)   kangofu   KⓐhN-GⓄ-FⓄⓄ

O

ocean   umi   ⓄⓄ-MⒺE

October   jūgatsu   JⓄⓄ-GⓐhT-SⓄⓄ

one-way (traffic)   ippō tsūkō

  ⒺEP-PⓄ TSⓄⓄ-KⓄ

onion   tamanegi   Tⓐh-Mⓐh-Nⓔ̆-GⒺE

optician (an)   meganeya   Mⓔ̆-Gⓐh-Nⓔ̆-Yⓐh

orange (color) orenji O-REN-JEE

orange (fruit) orenji iro no

  O-REN-JEE EE-RO NO

order (to) chūmon suru CHOO-MON SOO-ROO

original orijinaru O-REE-JEE-Nah-ROO

oysters kaki Kah-KEE

P

package kozutsumi KO-ZOOT-SOO-MEE

paid haraimashita Hah-RI-Mah-SH-Tah

pain itami EE-Tah-MEE

pantyhose pantī stokkingu

  Pah N-TEE STOK-KEEN-GOO

paper kami Kah-MEE

passenger jōkyaku JO-KEE-ah-KOO

passport pasupōto Pah S-PO-TO

pasta pasuta Pah-SOO-Tah

pastries pēsutorī PA-SOO-TO-REE

pen pen PEN

pepper koshō KO-SHO

perfume kōsui KO-SOO-EE

person hito HEE-TO

pharmacist (a) yakuzaishi YAH-KOO-ZI-SHEE

pharmacy kusuriya KOO-SOO-REE-YAH

photo shashin SHAH-SHEEN

photographer shashin SHAH-SHEEN

pie pai PI

pie (apple) appuru pai AHP-POO-ROO PI

pillow makura MAH-KOO-RAH

pink (color) pinku PEEN-KOO

pizza piza PEE-ZAH

plate (a) sara SAH-RAH

please (when offering) dōzo DO-ZO

please (when requesting) onegaishimasu
  O-NEH-GI-SHEE-MAHS

pleasure tanoshimi TAH-NO-SHEE-MEE

police keisatsu KA-SAHT-SOO

police station keisatsusho KA-SAHT-SOO-SHO

pork butaniku BOO-TAH-NEE-KOO

porter   pōtā   PO-Tah

post office   yūbinkyoku   YOO-BEEN-KEE-O-Koo

postcard   hagaki   Hah-Gah-KEE

potato   jagaimo   Jah-GI-MO

pregnant   ninshin chū   NEEN-SHEEN CHoo

prescription   shohōsen   SHO-HO-SeN

price   nedan   Ne-Dah N

problem   mondai   MON-DI

public   ōyake no   O-Yah-Ke NO

purple (color)   murasaki iro no

    Moo-Rah-Sah-KEE EE-RO NO

purse   handobaggu   Hah N-DO-BahG-Goo

Q

question   shitsumon   SHEET-Soo-MON

quick (fast)   hayai   Hah-YI

quiet   shizuka na   SHEE-Zoo-Kah Nah

R

radio   rajio   Rah-JEE-O

rain   ame   @h-M&

raincoat   rein kōto   ℝ@N K◎-T◎

ramp (a)   keisha-ro   K@-SH@h-ℝ◎

rare (meat)   rea no   ℝ&-@h N◎

razor blade   kamisori no ha

   K@h-M&-S◎-ℝ&   N◎ H@h

ready   yōi ga dekimashita

   Y◎-&   G@h   D&-K&-M@SH-T@h

receipt   reshīto   ℝ&-SH&-T◎

recommend (to)   suisen suru

   S◎◎-&-S&N   S◎◎-ℝ◎◎

red (color)   akai   @h-K①

repeat (it)   mō ichido   M◎   &-CH&-D◎

reservation   yoyaku   Y◎-Y@h-K◎◎

restaurant   resutoran   ℝ&S-T◎-ℝ@hN

return (to)   kaeru   K@h-&-ℝ◎◎

   (come back)   kaerimasu   K@h-&-ℝ&-M@hS

rice (cooked)   gohan   G◎-H@hN

rich   kanemochina   K@h-N&-M◎-CH&-N@h

right (correct)   tadashii   Tah-Dah-SHEE

right (direction)   migi   MEE-GEE

road   michi   MEE-CHEE

room   heya   HĕE-Yah

round trip   ōfuku   O-Foo-Koo

S

safe (valuables)   kinko   KEEN-KO

salad   sarada   Sah-Rah-Dah

sale   sēru   SA-Roo

salmon   shake   SHah-Kĕ

salt   shio   SHEE-O

sandwich   sandoitchi   Sah N-DO-EET-CHEE

Saturday   doyōbi   DO-YO-REE

seafood   shīfūdo   SHEE-Foo-DO

seat   seki   Sĕ-KEE

secretary   hisho   HEE-SHO

September   kugatsu   Koo Gah T-Soo

service   sābisu   Sah-BEE-Soo

shampoo   shanpū   SHah N-Poo

shirt   waishatsu   WI-SHah T-Soo

shoes kutsu   KOOT-SOO

shoe store kutsuya   KOOT-SOO-Yah

shopping shoppingu   SHOP-PEEN-GOO

shower shawā   SHah-Wah

shrimp ebi   e-BEE

sick byōki   BEE-O-KEE

signature shomei   SHO-MI

single (marital status)   dokushin

  DO-KOO SHEEN

sister shimai   SHEE-MI

size saizu   SI-ZOO

skin hifu   HEE-FOO

skirt sukāto   SOO-Kah-TO

sleeves sode   SO-De

slowly yukkurito   YOOK-KOO-REE-TO

small chiisai   CHEE-SI

smoke (to)   tabako o suu   Tah-Bah-KO O SOO

soap sekken   SeK-KeN

socks kutsushita   KOOT-SOO-SHEE-Tah

soon sugu Soo-Goo

soup sūpu Soo-Poo

south minami MEE-Nah-MEE

spoon supūn SPooN

sport supōtsu Soo-POT-Soo

spring (season) haru Hah-Roo

stair kaidan KI-Dah-N

stamps kitte KEE-T-Te

station (train) eki e-KEE

steak stēki STA-KEE

steamed mushita Moo-SHEE-Tah

stop! tomete! TO-Me-Te

store omise O-MEE-Se

strawberries ichigo EE-CHEE-GO

street michi MEE-CHEE

subway chikatetsu CHEE-Kah-TeT-Soo

sugar satō Sah-TO

suit (clothes) sūtsu SooT-Soo

suitcase sūtsu kēsu SooT-Soo Ke-Soo

summer   natsu   N@T-S⊙⊙

sunglasses   san-guras   S@N-G⊙⊙-Ɓ@S

suntan oil   santan oiru   S@N-T@N   ⊙y-Ɓ⊙⊙

Sunday   nichiyōbi   N©-CH©-Y⊙-Ɓ©

swim (to)   oyogu   ⊙-Y⊙-G⊙⊙

swimming pool   pūru   P⊙⊙-Ɓ⊙⊙

synagogue   yudaya kyō no jiin

   Y⊙⊙-D@-Y@   KY⊙   N⊙   J©N

T

table   tēburu   Tẽ-Ɓ⊙⊙-Ɓ⊙⊙

tampon   tanpon   T@N-P⊙N

tape (sticky)   serotēpu   Sẽ-Ɓ⊙-T@-P⊙⊙

tape recorder   tēpu rekōdā

   T@-P⊙⊙   Ɓẽ-K⊙-D@

tax   zeikin   Z@-K©N

taxi   takushī   T@K-SH©

tea   cha   CH@

telephone   denwa   DẽN-W@

television   terebi   Tẽ-Ɓẽ-Ɓ©

temperature ondo ON-DO

temple otera U-TE-Rah

tennis tenisu TE-NEE-Soo

tennis court tenisu kōto

TEN-NEE-Soo KO-TO

thank you dōmo arigatō

DO-MO ah-REE-Gah-TO

that (see page 23)

the (not used in Japanese)

there asoko ah-SO-KO

they (see page 23)

this (see page 23)

throat nodo NO-DO

Thursday mokuyōbi MO-Koo-YO-BEE

ticket kippu KEEP-Poo

tie (neck tie) nekutai NE-Koo-TIE

time jikan JEE-Kahn

tip (gratuity) chippu CHEEP-Poo

tire taiya TIE-Yah

tobacco   tabako   T(ah)-B(ah)-K(O)

today   kyō   K(EE)-(O)

toilet paper   toiretto pēpā

  T(oy)-R(eh)T-T(O)   P(A)-P(ah)

tomato   tomato   T(O)-M(ah)-T(O)

toothbrush   haburashi   H(ah)-B(oo)-R(ah)-SH(EE)

toothpaste   nerihamigaki

  N(eh)-R(EE)-H(ah)-M(EE)-G(ah)-K(EE)

toothpick   yōji   Y(O)-J(EE)

tour   kankō   K(ah)N-K(O)

tourist   kankō kyaku   K(ah)N-K(O)   K(EE)-(ah)-K(oo)

towel   taoru   T(ah)-(O)-R(oo)

train   densha   D(eh)N-SH(ah)

travel agency   ryokōdairiten

  R(EE)-(O)-K(O)-D(I)-R(EE)-T(eh)N

traveler's check   torabērah chēk-ku

  T(O)-R(ah)-B(eh)-R(ah)   CH(eh)K-K(oo)

trip   ryokō   R(EE)-(O)-K(O)

trousers   zubon   Z(oo)-B(O)N

trout masu Mah-Soo

Tuesday kayōbi Kah-YO-BEE

tuna maguro Mah-Goo-RO

turkey shichimenchō SHEE-CHEE-MEN-CHO

U

umbrella kasa Kah-Sah

understand (to) wakaru Wah-Kah-Roo

underwear shitagi SHEE-Tah-GEE

United States Gash-Shūkoku

   GahSH-SHOO-KO-KOO

up ue (ni) oo-e (NEE)

urgent shikyū SHEE-KYoo

V

vacant kara no Kah-Bah NO

vacation bakēshon Bah-K-A-SHON

valuable daijina DI-JEE-Nah

veal ko-ushi KO-oo-SHEE

vegetables yasai Yah-SI

view nagame Nah-Gah-ME

vinegar su S◎◎

vinegar and oil su to oiru S◎◎ T◎ ◎ʸ-Ⓡ◎◎

W

wait! chotto matte! CHⓄ-TⓄ MⓐT-Tⓔ

waiter uētā WⒶ-Tⓐʰ

waitress uēitoresu WⒶ-TⓄ-Ⓡⓔ-S◎◎

wash (to) arau ⓐʰ-Ⓡⓐʰ-◎◎ (araimasu)
ⓐʰ-ⓇⒾ-Mⓐʰ S

watch (clock store) tokeiya TⓄ-KⒾ-Yⓐʰ

watch (wrist) ude dokei ◎◎-Dⓔ DⓄ-KⒾ

water (drinking) nomi mizu NⓄ-Mⓔⓔ Mⓔⓔ-Z◎◎

watermelon suika S◎◎-ⓔⓔ-Kⓐʰ

we watashitachi wa Wⓐʰ-Tⓐʰ-SHⓔⓔ-Tⓐʰ-CHⓔⓔ-Wⓐʰ

weather tenki TⓔN-Kⓔⓔ

Wednesday suiyōbi S◎◎-ⓔⓔ-YⓄ-Ⓑⓔⓔ

week (this) konshū KⓄN-SH◎◎

welcome (to) kangei suru KⓐN-GⒾ S◎◎-Ⓡ◎◎

well done weru dān Wⓔ-Ⓡ◎◎ DⓐʰN

west nishi Nⓔⓔ-SHⓔⓔ

wheelchair kurumaisu KOO-ROO-MAH-EE-SOO

when? itsu? EET-SOO

where? doko? DO-KO

white shiroi SHEE-RO-EE

wife (your) kani KAH-NEE

wife (someone else's) okusan O-KOO-SAHN

wine wain WINE

winter fuyu FOO-YOO

woman onna ON-NAH

wonderful subarashii SOO-BAH-RAH-SHEE

wrong warui WAH-ROO-EE

XYZ

x-ray rentogen REN-TO-GEN

year nen NEN

yellow kiiroi KEE-RO-EE

yes hai HI

you anata ah-NAH-TAH

zipper jippā JEEP-PAH

zoo dōbutsuen DO-BOOT-SOO-EN

THANKS!

The nicest thing you can say to anyone in any language is "Thank you." Try some of these languages using the incredible EPLS Vowel Symbol System.

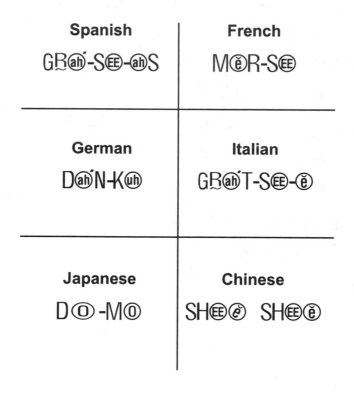

Spanish	French
GR**ah**-S**EE**-**ah**S	M**ĕ**R-S**EE**

German	Italian
D**ah**N-K**uh**	GR**ah**T-S**EE**-**ĕ**

Japanese	Chinese
D**O**-M**O**	SH**EE**-**ĕ** SH**EE**-**ĕ**

Swedish	**Portuguese**
T(ah)K	(O)-BR(EE)-G(ah)-D(O)
Arabic	**Greek**
SH(oo)-KR(ah)N	(e)F-H(ah)-R(EE)-ST(O)´
Hebrew	**Russian**
T(O)-D(ah)´	SP(ah)-S(EE)-B(ah)
Swahili	**Dutch**
(ah)-S(ah)´N-T(A)	D(ah)NK (oo)
Tagalog	**Hawaiian**
S(ah)-L(ah)-M(ah)´T	M(ah)-H(ah)´-L(O)

INDEX

NOTES

QUICK REFERENCE PAGE

Good morning (polite)
Ohayō gozaimasu
O-Hah-YO GO-ZI-MahS

Hello / Good afternoon	**Good-bye**
Konnichi wa	Sayōnara
KON-NEE-CHEE Wah	Sah-YO-Nah-Rah

Yes	**No**
Hai	Iie
HI	E -ĕ

Please (when asking for things)	**Please** (go ahead)
...o kudasai	Dōzo
...O KOO-Dah-SI	DO -ZO

Thank you
Dōmo arigatō
DO -MO ah-REE-Gah-TO

I would like...	**Where?**
... o kudasai	Doko desu ka?
...O KOO-Dah-SI	DO-KO DĕS-Kah

I don't understand!	**Help!**
Wakarimasen!	Tasukete!
Wah-Kah-REE-Mah-SĕN	Tah-S-Kĕ-Tĕ

166